THE CAUSES OF WAR

THE CAUSES OF WAR

ECONOMIC, INDUSTRIAL, RACIAL, RELIGIOUS, SCIENTIFIC, AND POLITICAL

BY

SIR ARTHUR SALTER · SIR J. ARTHUR THOMSON
G. A. JOHNSTON · ALFRED ZIMMERN
C. F. ANDREWS · FREDERICK J. LIBBY
HENRY A. ATKINSON · WICKHAM STEED
AND OTHERS

AS RAPPORTEURS OF THE VARIOUS SECTIONS OF
COMMISSION I. OF THE WORLD CONFERENCE FOR
INTERNATIONAL PEACE THROUGH RELIGION—
AS SUBMITTED TO THE EXECUTIVE COMMITTEE
FOR PRESENTATION TO THE WORLD CONFERENCE

WITH INTRODUCTION BY
RUTH CRANSTON

EDITED BY
ARTHUR PORRITT

Essay Index Reprint Series

BOOKS FOR LIBRARIES PRESS
FREEPORT, NEW YORK

First Published 1932
Reprinted 1969

JX
1930
.W61
A5
1969

STANDARD BOOK NUMBER:
8369-1372-8

LIBRARY OF CONGRESS CATALOG CARD NUMBER:
70-99719

PRINTED IN THE UNITED STATES OF AMERICA

CONTENTS

SUPPLEMENTARY

MEMBERS OF COMMISSION I. OF THE WORLD CONFERENCE FOR INTERNATIONAL PEACE THROUGH RELIGION

Mr. A. Yusuf Ali
Mr. C. F. Andrews
Dr. J. Ayusawa
Dr. Moritz Bonn
Dr. Martin Buber
Prof. C. Delisle Burns
Dr. John B. Carruthers
Dr. W. C. Chen
Dame Rachel Crowdy
Mr. Jackson Fleming
Mrs. Jackson Fleming
Father Haas
Dr. H. Hartmann
Professor Heyde
Prof. W. J. Hinton
Baroness O. van Hogendorp
Mr. J. Hugh Jackson
Mr. G. A. Johnston
Pasteur Georges Lauga
Prof. F. Maurette
Pastor Mensching
The Rt. Hon. Lord Olivier
Mr. E. J. Phelan
Prof. André Philip
Mr. H. S. L. Polak
Sir J. Arthur Salter
Mr. T. R. V. Sastri
The Rt. Hon. V. S. Srinivasa Sastri
Prof. André Siegfried
Dr. Rabindranath Tagore
Dr. Georges Thélin
Prof. A. Titius
Dr. Jacob Viner
Dr. Kuangson Young
Sir Francis Younghusband

INTRODUCTION

By Ruth Cranston
(Secretary of the Commission)

THE Executive Committee of the World Conference for International Peace through Religion decided to organise the Conference along the lines of four international Commissions.

Commission No. 1.—"What are the causes of war and the tendencies that make for war?"

Economic	Racial	Press and Propaganda
Industrial	Political	

Commission No. 2.—"What are the spiritual forces with which these influences can be met?"

Religious	Cultural	Philanthropic
Scientific	Educational	

Commission No. 3.—"What is being done by the religions and religious associations throughout the world in the cause of international peace?"

Commission No. 4.—"How can we mobilise the spiritual forces of the world to do away with war and to ensure peace?"

Commissions 2, 3, and 4 of this scheme have to do with matters for which religious people may be supposed to have some natural equipment.

When it came, however, to the organisation of *Commission* 1—the basis for the discussion and decisions that should follow—it was felt that the reports to be prepared on economic, industrial, racial, and political causes of war should be entrusted not to the inexperienced members of our own organisation, but to experts in these several fields: men and women who have the requisite knowledge and who could present it with precision and authority. It was decided to endeavour to interest such persons in the organisation of the Commission along these lines, and it is only necessary to look at the list of distinguished men making up the membership of the Commission, to realise the gratifying response to this effort.

The Committee wishes to express its appreciation of the more than generous help and cooperation accorded us by these tremendously busy people, whom we invited to assist in this work. Beset by calls and commitments on all sides, they yet found time and energy to include this one more task in their already heavy programmes, because, many of them said, they felt that the religious forces of the world are so important in the education of public opinion, and because there has never been a survey of causes of war on such a scale as this Conference is undertaking. People like Sir Arthur Salter, Professor De Madariaga, Professor Siegfried, Dr. Bonn, and others of similar distinction, laid aside other work, or gave part of their holiday period to attend meetings and make their contributions to this Commission. The results are embodied in the reports which compose this book. The Committee believes that it will be generally agreed that they

constitute a remarkable set of documents, well
worth careful study, both on their individual
merits and as a collective whole.

Four more sections have been added to the
Commission, besides those originally listed. Certain members of the Commission felt that the
spiritual influences of the world (being positively
studied under *Commission* 2) could be used negatively, and are frequently so used—as influences
that make *for* war. It was thought, therefore,
that brief studies of these in their negative aspect
should be included in the report of *Commission* 1.
Thus the report includes Religious, Scientific,
Cultural, and Educational (Press and Propaganda) causes of war, as well as Economic,
Industrial, Racial, and Political causes.

In preparation for these reports, there was first
informal discussion by sections. Then a draft
report was prepared by one or more members of
the section. This was sent round for criticism and
suggestion by other members. The present reports have been revised in the light of these
criticisms and suggestions, and may therefore be
said to represent the ideas of the section as a
whole, and not simply of one or two individuals.

In a survey of the finished documents, what
appears to us most impressive is the identity of
the principles now urgently preached by experts
in practical affairs, with the principles always
preached by the great religious teachers. At the
preliminary meeting of the World Conference for
International Peace through Religion, held in
Geneva in 1928, it was clearly shown by representatives of the eleven great religions that the
ideals or principles taught by every one of the

great Masters and founders of religion are the
same: namely, human solidarity, unity of life,
interests, destiny—co-operation, instead of competition, as the guiding rule of life; help, instead
of exploitation of the weak and backward.

These are the principles taught by every great
religious seer. They are also the principles taught
by every good modern economist and political
and industrial authority. Far from being considered "mystic" and "impractical" to-day, these
principles are acknowledged as the only practical
bases on which the modern world can be run.
The World Economic Conference, Labour Office
reports, the statements of bankers, lawyers, and
business men all over the globe, reiterate this
increasingly evident fact.

But the fact has not yet become apparent to
the average individual, or the central and controlling principle in the public mind. And it is
here that we believe the religious and educative
forces have their opportunity. The reports given
out to the public through the various international offices at Geneva and elsewhere have
been necessarily technical reports—and reports
in sections: reports of economic and financial
commissions, of commissions, on social work,
hygiene, and so on. They have been largely
negative analyses of what was wrong, with certain recommendations for each department as to
how these wrongs could be righted. Each report
has made a valuable contribution, but it has
little effect beyond the limits of the small group
professionally interested in the specific questions.
It remains for some agency to gather together
all these different studies and recommendations

into a co-ordinated and synthesised whole, and
to present it to the world as a positive picture
and ideal of what life to-day could be, in a
world more sanely organised, and to indicate
ways and means whereby the ideal can be
realised.

Without a vision the people to-day—in every
country—*are* perishing. They lack the inspiration,
the driving force of a great desire, and the possibility of its fulfilment, to spur them on. All the
talk is about war and peace. But what people
want is peace, not in the static but in the positive
sense: freedom, security, to develop their individual powers, and a more satisfying life
generally. How can we get this freedom? How
can we realise the sort of world we wish, instead
of the suspicious threatening world we have?

The reports of these Commissions, it is hoped,
will throw some light on this great subject.

SUMMARY

Sir Arthur Salter

The most convenient classification of the principal causes of wars as we see them to have arisen in history is: 1. Religious; 2. Dynastic; 3. Political; and 4. Economic.

It is obvious that these causes may be, and often have been, combined.

As the cause of a single war there may be a complex of dynastic, economic, religious, and political activities.

The relative importance of these causes, and the proportions in which they combine to form a dangerous amalgam, differ enormously at different stages of the world's history and different parts of the world's surface.

For countries of an Occidental civilisation, religious conflicts, for some centuries the principal cause of devastating wars, have ceased to be a danger which we need consider.

In Oriental countries there are still instances in which religious rivalries may menace peace.

On the whole, it may justly be said that, at this stage of the world's history, the natural rôle of the forces of religion is to assist the cause of peace, not to threaten it.

"Dynastic" causes may be briefly dismissed.

The third category, "political" causes, obviously cannot be similarly dismissed.

Nationalist movements, the grievances of Irredentist minorities, the explosions that arise from alleged affronts to national dignity and honour fall within this category. It is perhaps true that at this moment causes of this kind present the most obvious, direct, and immediate threat to peaceful relations.

The political and the economic motives are intertwined beyond the hope of disentanglement.

In present conditions in Europe a country is unlikely to initiate or threaten war to secure an economic result, but an enduring sense of economic grievance may inflame a general national antagonism to the point of imminent danger. It is very easy, but very unwise, to neglect the more deep-rooted and enduring cause for the one which, especially when danger is imminent, is the more obvious.

The political factor is perhaps more important than the economic.

In the dangers to a breach of the peace, therefore, political factors are now most prominent, and are likely to be so for some time to come.

Future peace depends not only upon the character of the preventive machinery, but also upon whether the normal life of the world is, or is not, such as to create deep and intensely felt divergencies of policy and interest.

If the preventive machinery, aided by war memories and war weariness, can prevent the present political resentments from causing another war for a substantial time, the specifically political forces which make for danger should tend to diminish.

On any reasonably long view of the future, the preventive machinery against war is likely to prevent purely political causes from leading to war unless they are reinforced by economic conflicts of interest and policy.

The characteristic form of the present and probable economic conflicts is not to be found in attempts to acquire new territory. It is to be found in the use of the power of government to deflect the course of trade between one country or another.

The principal classes of cases in which Governments intervene or may intervene in economic competition, and so cause the dangers to international relations are: (1) Commercial Policy; (2) Population Problems; (3) Credit, Currency and Capital Problems; (4) Transportation Problems; (5) Raw Material Problems; (6) Diplomacy in Relation to Competition; (7) Internal Social Trouble and its Political Reactions.

Countries do not normally regard themselves as having a

natural right to free entry into each other's markets. It is
very different, however, if they are deprived, especially
suddenly, of a right previously enjoyed for a long period;
if large and important industries which have grown up in
response to a trade demand made possible by free entry or
low tariffs are suddenly dislocated or destroyed by new
duties.

In contrast with tariffs, State-aided dumping causes an
amount of friction altogether out of proportion to its
economic effect.

It is the combination of State association and dumping
that is serious.

If explosions are to be prevented, the peoples of the world
must work positively and co-operatively at finding a safety-
valve for the explosive forces, and not merely defensively
at national policies designed to direct the explosion elsewhere.

The most dangerous form of loan is that which is regarded
at first as a purely private transaction, negotiated by
private persons with the borrowing Government, without
regard to political considerations, but which afterwards,
when default occurs, proves to involve such interests as to
result in governmental action.

If the raw materials are available on equal terms to the
whole world, the sovereignty over the territory in which
they are produced is obviously of much less importance to
international relations than if it were used to give a competitive advantage to the industry of a particular country.
Dangers from this source are not imminent at present,
because more and not less materials, of practically every
kind, are being produced than industry needs; and because,
largely for this reason, competition in their sale secures equal
and easy conditions for all importing countries.

It follows that this is a specially favourable period in
which to try to secure agreement as to the principles which
should permanently govern the supply of raw materials to
other countries than those which need them. For it is much
easier to prevent than to terminate provocative and
preferential practices.

A little recognised, but important, source of friction in
international relations arises from the use of the diplomatic
machine to assist nationals in economic competition.

What is most needed is effective world agreement as to the principles which should guide Governments in the action they take affecting the economic interests of other countries, and therefore international relations.

G. A. Johnston

It is probable that no great war was ever due to a single cause. Wars are rather the result of a group of causes, the most apparent of which are not always the most fundamental. The fundamental causes of war are usually to be found in the slow development of tendencies and policies which may begin to develop for years, and even for generations, before the actual explosion takes place.

All influences inimical to the realisation of social justice are influences dangerous to the maintenance of peace.

When a country is aware that the pressure of population is becoming too great to be supported in accordance with previously applied methods of utilising its resources, it has so far found in general two, and only two, solutions to this problem. One is emigration, the other is intensive industrialisation. By a curious fatality, action in accordance with either one or the other of these solutions is apt to bring the State into conflict with other Powers.

The problem of Manchuria, which is regarded in Pacific countries as the most dangerous part of the world's surface from the point of view of the possibility of future war, is essentially connected with the necessity of the development of industrialism in Japan.

If it is admitted that the material basis of the welfare of the community is improved as a result of mechanisation, what of the individual producers themselves, the workers whose functions are largely reduced to those of machine tenders?

Even if it be admitted that monotony is not felt to result from the actual repetitive process so much as from the general atmosphere of the factory, and even if it be further agreed that monotony is not an objective quality of things but a subjective feeling of persons, it must be maintained that the monotony involved in the constitution of the industrial order has real importance from the standpoint of peace and war. For if work is merely repetitive and requires no concentrated effort of attention on the part of the

the community, a section in which all the evils of mob
psychology tend to develop. If in any country a large number of men are unemployed over long periods of time, these
sentiments of demoralisation and solidarity with the other
unemployed, embittered by the vision of the sufferings of
dependent women and children, obviously bear within them
the seeds of social catastrophe.

Bad conditions of work are of importance from the standpoint of war and peace because they naturally produce discontent and dissatisfaction.

The settlement of industrial disputes by means of strikes
and lock-outs is akin to the settlement of political disputes
by means of war.

It is clear that if a worker's conditions of life are so bad
that under no circumstances does it seem to him that they
can be worse, a particularly fruitful field is provided for the
artificial stimulation of mass movements of revolution.

The rigid discipline of modern industry renders impossible
during hours of work the expression of most of the instincts
and impulses natural to man.

Long hours of work, inimical to the full development of
family life, cannot be other than an influence making for
social instability.

Low wages have an influence on conditions making for
war not only in a national aspect, that is, not only in a
particular country, but also internationally and in connection with national differences in standards of living.

The general economic interdependence of the world has a
tendency to depress the standards of life of the worker in
industrially developed countries.

If the workers of a country become convinced that their
standard of living is low, and, further, that there is no possibility of securing an improvement in it because some other
country possesses the raw materials which they need or contains the empty territories on which they would like to
settle, or closes its markets to the goods they would like to
export, it needs no stretch of imagination to recognise that
they might readily be induced to attempt, by war, to obtain
what negotiation has failed to secure.

If the intensive study now being made by economists,
statisticians, bankers, and others, into the technique of world

economic balance through planning were more closely co-
ordinated, there can be little doubt that the world would.
devise measures for securing greater equilibrium between
its powers of consumption and its capacity to produce.

C. F. Andrews

In the present stage of human development, racial
differentiation, when not distorted or artificially excited,
has a necessary and important part to play which must on
no account be lost sight of. Therefore, while dealing with the
harm caused to mankind by acute racial animosity, we must
constantly remember that there are other aspects of "race"
which make for peace and goodwill and are therefore of the
highest value.

The consensus of opinion within the Commission is that
the race problem, owing to which world disturbances have
occurred, is primarily a political and economic problem
rather than a purely biological one. . . .

Races have been brought near to one another without any
preparation for mutual readjustment of standards of living.

The races of the East have begun bitterly to feel the
economic exploitation of the West.

Although it may be difficult in modern times to point to
wars that are purely racial in character—parallel to the
tribal wars in the past—yet it is evident to-day that the
racial factor is entering into and complicating situations
which are already overstrained, and thus tending very
seriously to endanger world peace.

Whenever this feeling of racial superiority enters along
with its correlative, racial inferiority, every outward
difference tends to become exaggerated on either side.

The ultimate problem of world peace has always been
how to break through these vicious circles and restore human
justice without recourse to violence.

Even though religious wars have not been practised in
during recent historic times, nevertheless the hostile sentiment still remains wherever the superiority of one religion
over another is emphasised in a sensational manner by
modern methods of propaganda, and where a more primitive
moral code is condemned by the intellectual standards of a
higher culture.

xxii THE CAUSES OF WAR

True historical and cultural appreciation should be encouraged by careful study. This should begin in the primary schools on both sides of the world, and a thorough revision of historical and geographical text-books should be undertaken.

The antipathy to Japan in America, which expressed itself bluntly and crudely in the Asiatic Exclusion Act of 1924 and also by continual instances of racial discrimination along the Pacific Coast of North America, has been resented with an intensity of feeling difficult to understand in the United States.

In recent times, owing to disturbed political conditions and the humiliation involved in subjection, Indians are beginning to be aware of a racial consciousness among themselves which cuts across the barriers of their own castes and creeds, putting national units first.

The gravest racial crisis in the present generation is met with in South Africa.

Central Africa is still in many respects, as a focus of racial evils, one of the darkest spots on the map of the world.

The full historical and scientific knowledge, which might throw light upon the racial problem at this point (the difficult and complicated question of race-mingling) where amateur opinion is so divided, has never yet been fully collected and explored. Yet all the while an explosive force is being generated within human society which flashes out in lawless acts, such as lynching, and gives rise to such organisations as the Ku-Klux-Klan.

Matters of very great moment, affecting the future of the human race, are being settled in a haphazard manner by the blind excitement of passion and greed rather than by reasonable actions based on mutual consideration and goodwill.

Since the future of the human race is likely still further to witness congestion of population, the careful teaching of each generation, in turn, as to the vital necessity of goodwill in dealing with the idiosyncrasies of other people, becomes of primary importance.

Textbooks used in schools which give a contemptuous or one-sided description of other races need to be carefully revised.

How incredibly short-sighted the present generation is, may easily be seen by the moving pictures which are being

sent from America and Europe all over the world giving
only the coarser side of Western civilisation.

Evidence has also been given to the Commission that in
Great Britain race relations have become less cordial since
the number of foreign students from the East has increased.

Efforts ought to be made from the side of the East to limit
the influx each year to students of mature age, who may
come to the West for research work and advanced study.

Inconsiderate racial treatment by Western people, which
once was taken passively, now is deeply resented. The old
superiority exercised by the Western Powers is no longer
acknowledged on the same scale. The prestige of the West
has broken down—partly as a result of the War—and its
influence over the masses of illiterate villagers in India and
elsewhere has passed away, never to be recalled.

It is a bounden duty at such critical times to plead
earnestly that the Christian Religion itself, along with other
religions also, has laid down the precept of daily conduct
whereby men should do to others what they would wish to be
done to themselves. This reciprocal treatment would surely
imply that national freedom in the East ought to be not less
dear to Western nations than their own freedom. Along the
line of this great principle of reciprocity—which is well
understood in the East—there is hope that the new uprising
of racial animosity may subside; but without this recognition, it is likely still further to increase.

The balance of wealth in the world is now heavily loaded
against the East, which has neither the machine-power, nor
the realised mineral wealth of the West. This leads to a false
sense of superiority on the part of the West and an altogether
unnecessary humiliation, in outward circumstances, on the
part of the East. This material inequality is felt all the more
bitterly because it is combined often with political subjection. The injustice of all this and a rankling sense of wrong
is one of the most potent causes of strife.

Political control has led to an economic imperialism of an
oppressive character, whereby the stronger power by its
material resources and scientific equipment is able to exploit
for its own use the weakness of the East.

All influences producing social injustice imperil the cause
of world peace.

Clearly nothing could less express the spirit and character

of Christ than any exhibition of racial arrogance among those who go out to preach in His name. In spite of the presence in the mission field of exceptional characters, leading lives of great simplicity and humility, and thus truly representing their Master, there are still to be found among missionaries those who have greatly embittered Eastern minds by ignorant attacks and foolish controversy, and also by an assumed superiority that provokes all who have come in contact with it. The cause of World Peace through Religion becomes endangered when the representatives of religion themselves provoke ill-will and strife.

No single action would do more to remove at one stroke grave suspicions and misapprehensions than the full and unconditional affirmation of racial equality at the very centre of international action.

Henry A. Atkinson

Religion has been, in the past, one of the most fruitful causes of war.

The quarrel among Christians themselves makes one of the blackest chapters in religious history.

Whole nations and groups of nations, utilising religious sentiment, have plunged into war and heroically sustained the more frightful havoc following war through the religious enthusiasm engendered.

Every war at some period, if it lasted long enough, became a "Holy War".

A deeper study and a truer analysis will convince anyone that there have been very few purely religious wars; that is, wars fought solely for religion and in the interests of religion.

This question may, with profit, be raised: Can religion, that plays such an important part in human life, be made as strong a factor for peace as it has been for war?

A. Yusuf Ali

The Hindu-Muslim differences in India cannot really be classified as among the causes likely to lead to war . . . which is a matter between organised States.

Hinduism and Islam, in their basic ideas, are not necessarily antagonistic.

Sir J. Arthur Thomson

In the strict sense, of course, it is not science as such that is to blame, but our imperfect human nature that uses knowledge for evil purposes.

There is considerable evidence in support of the view that the Conflict of Races has had some useful influence in the evolution of civilisation.

We have maintained (1) that discovery is not to blame for the abuse of inventions based on it; (2) that if an appeal is made to science, it must be to the science of living beings as well as to the science of things and forces, and to the science of societies as well as to biology; (3) that established science is not to be blamed for the penumbra of opinion around unsolved problems, nor for the admixture of prejudice and metaphysics that is apt to be involved in the exposition of conclusions arrived at in the less exact fields; and (4) that mistakes are made by science, which are apt to be seized upon by those who seek for "good reasons" for their reversionary promptings.

Alfred Zimmern

It is culture as an *occasion* rather than as a *cause* of war with which we shall be concerned.

Modern imperialism, in the interests of the same civilisation, has constantly resorted to violence and warfare in order to replace primitive by more modern and effective forms of government and administration. And within our own Western industrial communities compulsion has become a recognised instrument of social policy in establishing new habits and standards of living, and in assimilating backward portions of the community into the larger central mass.

Culture becomes a cause of war when the representatives of a superior culture, possessing also superior power, employ that power to impose their culture upon an inferior party.

Is the superior culture, when it is also superior in physical power, justified in intervening by force in putting down evil practices and rescuing the oppressed?

We can say, then, that the resort to war, by an individual Government, even against a slave-power whose barbarous practices are clearly proved and admitted, is no longer to be

held justifiable. It is for the international community to lay
down general rules, forbidding slavery and other indefensible social practices, and to enforce such rules by appropriate means. In other words, the vague terms "superior"
and "inferior" should be replaced by a definite list of practices which are so clearly "inferior" that, like illiteracy in
Western Europe, they are destined to be abolished by
governmental action.

If we admit this principle, which we may define as the
principle of International Cultural Minimum, we shall find
it easier to face the problem involved in the use of forms of
compulsion falling short of actual warfare or violence.

The right starting-point for the modern conscience in
dealing with our problem is the acceptance of the principle
that, just as all men are equal in the sight of God, so all
cultures are equal in the international community: all are
entitled to equal consideration: the members of all are
entitled to equal respect.

The principle of equality of cultures before the law rescues
the so-called inferior from the domain of philanthropy and
sets them side by side with their equals in the realm of
international social policy.

To make participation in a particular culture the criterion
of membership of a State is to destroy the meaning of law,
the glory of which is to be common to men as men, and to
obliterate the distinction between public and private, between the realm of Caesar and the realm of the spirit.

Men must learn, in Europe as elsewhere, to think of the
state as an organisation transcending and ignoring the
idiosyncrasies of this or that social group in its effort to provide the means of good living for them all. They must learn
to think of law as the agent, not of the decrees of a particular set of rulers who happen to occupy the seats of power
but of the intelligence, will, and conscience of diverse and
miscellaneous human beings united in a community and in
social service for the public good. And they must come to
realise that, if the waging of war in the name of religion is
the darkest stain on the pages of the Christian record, the
superiority-complex which invokes the name of culture in
its service, whether for open warfare or for secret humiliation, is a sin comparable to that of those of whom it was
said that it were better that a millstone were hanged about

their neck and that they were drowned in the depth of the
sea.

Frederick J. Libby

There is no question that if the owners and editors and
reporters of the Press of the world decided to use their
power to establish peace they could do it.

Powerful individual papers have been the decisive influence on different occasions in actually bringing about a
war and in preventing wars.

The real question is how can news of a military nature,
inevitable and legitimate so long as the war machine exists,
be offset by news which will tend to create the newer picture
of a world organised on a peace basis.

In Europe there is much closer control over the Press than
in the United States. In several countries news agencies
are actually Government-owned or controlled, and a definite
censorship of the Press exists. Such manipulation of the
Press for political purposes as this control makes possible,
is from point of view, a grave danger.

Unless it is to be subjected to the absolute control of a
central authority, it is as misleading to speak of "the Press"
as it is to talk about "women".

Accepting the Press as it is, there are certain factors which
tend to make it an aid in establishing better international
relations and which should, therefore, be developed; and
there are certain others needing to be discouraged, since
their tendency is to throw the influence of the Press on the
side of the maintenance of the old war system.

Public recognition of the influence and power of members
of the newspaper profession: their more frequent inclusion
at least as advisors and consultants in public undertakings
in any community will also tend to call into the profession
men prepared for leadership.

Training in how to read the newspapers, what difficulties
in their compilation must be allowed for, by what internal
evidence prejudice in their columns can be detected, how
daily news can be supplemented with the longer discussions
to be found in magazines or in what amounts to a new type
of book, "the news book", dealing with current affairs,
should be given not only in colleges but in high schools

and, in so far as possible, in elementary schools, for it is the foundation of intelligent citizenship. The newspaper has its own task and function. There is no justification in making it, as it were, the scapegoat for virtues which it is the responsibility of the rest of the community to cultivate.

Wickham Steed

Undeniably, fear stands foremost among the conceivable causes of future war. It enters as largely into the outlook of Germany and of Soviet Russia as into that of Poland and France. Its removal is one of the major postulates of peace.

While no Government in Europe, perhaps no Government in the world, desires war, many apprehend that, somehow, war will break out.

The truth seems to be that even the international engagements directed against the recurrence of war have outrun the normal convictions of the peoples in whose names those engagements were entered into.

The problem of removing the causes of war is, in large measure, the problem of finding ways of enlisting men's passions not only against war itself but in the service of a new ideal of constructive human civilisation from which war "as an instrument of national policy" shall have been banned as foolish, barbaric, and unworthy.

Were it possible to spread information of unquestioned accuracy upon all questions that bear upon international relations, and to secure for such information unhesitating acceptance by all whom it may concern, the risk that emotional explosions may be brought about by propaganda or, to give it its true name, by partial and deliberately misleading statements, would be greatly diminished.

By dint of discussion, "security" has come to mean the political and territorial safety of France, and of the nations allied with her, against attack from outside. No analysis of the political causes of war can avoid a frank examination of this issue.

The feeling of insecurity, and the fears which it engenders, are undoubtedly the strongest potential causes of war in the world to-day. No nation, whether it belong to the League or not, and no signatory of the Paris Peace Pact, can be certain that, if it reduces its armaments to a point at which it would have to rely upon the help of others for defence against attack, such help would really be forthcoming. It cannot even be sure that the attacking nation would be effectively outlawed and opposed by the rest of the world.

Since war as an instrument of national policy has been renounced and, by renunciation, ostracised; since armaments cannot lawfully be used save in self-defence or in collective action against a law-breaker, their lawful function is no other than a police function, individually or jointly discharged, in the service of an international law which the outlawry of war has revolutionised.

The postulate of international, as of social, peace is that the law should be, and should be known to be, strong and strongly supported by public feeling. When this postulate has been fulfilled, the political causes of war will disappear, and the path of mankind will run towards the highest and hardest task men have ever essayed—the creation of peace.

THE CAUSES OF WAR

I

THE ECONOMIC CAUSES OF WAR

By SIR ARTHUR SALTER

THE occasions of war are innumerable; but the causes fall easily into a very few categories. It is convenient for many purposes to distinguish them by their main groups. But it may in some respects be misleading, because in practice different causes are usually combined and interact the one with the other. Subject to this caution, the most convenient classification of the principal causes of wars as we see them to have arisen in history is: 1. Religious; 2. Dynastic; 3. Political; and 4. Economic. Wars have been waged because a people professing one religion have desired to impose it on another; or because a monarch whose territories were primarily a family possession, acquired and transmissible by marriage and heredity, desired to augment them; or for "political" purposes (which we will define in a moment); or to secure economic advantages. It is obvious that these causes may be, and often have been, combined. A monarch has, for example, invaded a country whose economic resources he coveted, basing his claims upon hereditary family rights, inflaming the ardour of his subjects by an appeal

1   B

to their religion, and taking as his occasion either an alleged affront to national dignity or the political grievances of an Irredentist minority. That is, as the cause of a single war, there may be a complex of dynastic, economic, religious, and political motives.

Nevertheless, these four causes, however they may combine or interact, are in essence different; and, though this particular classification is neither final nor exhaustive, it is useful to distinguish them.

Now it is obvious, at once, that the relative importance of these causes, and the proportions in which they combine to form a dangerous amalgam, differ enormously at different stages of the world's history and different parts of the world's surface.

For countries of an Occidental civilisation, religious conflicts, for some centuries the principal cause of devastating wars, have ceased to be a danger which we need consider. Differences of religious belief in these countries continue. But they are mitigated by a certain sense of a common opposition to the forces of irreligion, and they are purged of any element of danger to peace by the recognition of the futility of a forcibly imposed religion. In oriental countries there are still instances in which religious rivalries may menace peace. But even in these the dominant aspect of a dangerous conflict is often, though not always, racial or national antagonism (into which rivalry in religion enters as an element). On the whole it may justly be said that, at this stage of the world's history, the natural rôle of the forces of religion is to assist the cause of peace, not to threaten it.

"Dynastic" causes may be briefly dismissed. Monarchs remain, but with diminished authority and with a much restricted area of the world under their control. Most of them are now rather public servants and representatives of their people than autocrats subordinating their countries' policies to their personal or dynastic interests. The caprice of dictators is perhaps the modern equivalent of dynastic ambitions as a danger to peace; but their area is circumscribed.

The third category, "political" causes, obviously cannot be similarly dismissed. The term is here used to comprise all the ideas, sentiments, and ambitions that touch national pride and national prestige, and also the desire of peoples to be governed by those of their own race rather than by aliens. Nationalist movements, the grievances of Irredentist minorities, the explosions that arise from alleged affronts to national dignity and honour fall within this category. It is perhaps true that at this moment causes of this kind present the most obvious, direct, and immediate threat to peaceful relations. If we look to the danger spots of Europe, to the relations between Poland and Germany, or Germany and France, or Italy and Jugoslavia, or Hungary in relation to Czechoslovakia or Roumania, we find the dominant aspect of the situation a political one; it is rather a nationalistic than an economic ambition that first meets the eye. To some extent, however, such an impression would be misleading. Often an economic conflict underlies what is apparently a political estrangement. In Poland and Germany, for example, while there is serious political animosity, it is largely kept alive by a conflict between the interests of rival coal-owners or pig-breeders. An intense and concentrated conflict of pecuniary interest uses a more widely spread and general racial antagonism which might otherwise weaken with time and cease to be dangerous. The political and the economic motives are intertwined beyond the hope of disentanglement. Even where the more fundamental and more important cause of trouble is economic, the outward aspect, and the one most directly related to immediate danger, is nearly always political. In present conditions in Europe a country is unlikely to initiate or threaten war to secure an economic result, but an enduring sense of economic grievance may inflame a general national antagonism to the point of imminent danger. It is very easy, but very unwise, to neglect the more deep-rooted and enduring cause for the one which, especially when danger is imminent, is the more obvious.

In the present crisis in the Far East the underlying cause is obviously economic. Japan, with her surplus population penned in by restrictions on migration and impeded in her foreign trade, has reached a mood of desperation. In Europe, however, the political factors still count more in the immediate prospects of war and peace.

For this there are numerous reasons. We are still within less than fourteen years of the greatest war in history. For four years sentiments of racial and nationalistic hatred were both inflamed by the incidents of the struggle and deliberately exploited by those who wished to sustain a flagging will to fight in the peoples of their respective countries. Moreover, the Peace Treaties left new frontier adjustments and consequent grievances which, in several danger spots in Europe, keep vivid the flame of nationalism. There is another result of the war which is perhaps even more important. Many countries were left with an intense feeling of insecurity. The new Covenant of the League was a hope rather than a proved safeguard to which they were prepared to entrust the sole charge of their security. And in the last ten years we have seen two alternative and competing principles in operation. On the one hand is what we may call the "universal system", of which both the Covenant of the League and the Kellogg Pact are examples; on the other the "alliance" principle. Under the first each country relies upon the material or moral aid of the world, as a whole, in case of attack. Under the second it relies upon alliances or understandings with particular countries. In the next ten or twenty years, probably, the peace of the world depends chiefly upon which of these principles proves stronger—for ultimately they are incompatible. The criterion is simple. If trouble arises will the countries not directly involved say "We must stand by our friends"? or will they say "We must judge the issue by reference to the Covenant and Pact engagements. Which of the disputants has observed these engagements? Which has resorted to hostile action in breach of them? We must determine our action accordingly"? If the former proves stronger—or if even before the actual dispute arises each country fears that it may—Europe, at least, will gradually fall into two groups of hostile alliances. Competitive armaments will increase; national hatreds and national fears will be constantly inflamed, and sooner or later war must come. Now this process is, if we adopt our general classification, eminently a "political" one, though here again we must remember that economic conflicts will aggravate the trouble.

In the dangers to a breach of the peace, therefore, political factors are now most prominent in Europe though not in the Far Eastern situation. But if we take a longer view we shall see that the importance of the economic factor is likely to increase steadily, and ultimately to constitute the central problem of the peace of the world. The preventive machinery of Covenant and Pact, the network of treaties designed to prevent war, and to provide alternative methods for the settlement of conflicts, grows rapidly from year to year. Its adequacy depends mainly upon the play of two factors; on the one hand the strength which it can derive from the determined loyalty of those who have constructed and accepted it, and on the other the strain which deep divergencies of interest and policy may impose on it. We may perhaps say with some confidence that it should certainly suffice to prevent what may be called accidental or capricious wars, and to settle the casual and occasional disputes and conflicts that arise in the course of the world's business if deeper and more enduring forces are not involved. On the other hand, no possible machinery for the settlement of disputes without war can be strong enough to stand every conceivable strain. Future peace depends not only upon the character of the preventive machinery, but also upon whether the normal life of the

world is, or is not, such as to create deep
and intensely felt divergences of policy and
interest.

Now, as we have seen, the strain imposed upon
the system is likely in the immediate future in
Europe to come most obviously from political
reasons; from the fears as to security and
the competitive armaments which both express and increase them; the grievances of
minorities; the separation of nationals of the same
country by a corridor of intervening sovereignty;
the national ambitions that claim or deny parity
in armed forces as an expression of political
status; the associations of political friends as
against others outside the group; the competitive
diplomacy in such regions as the Balkans that
this process of group-forming provokes; the rival
political systems of democracy, dictatorship, and
Bolshevism with their external reactions; the
historical and sentimental resentments at the
transfer of territory to other sovereignties under
recent treaties, and so on.

As, however, the world settles down again to
its normal life, as memories of the war and its
immediate consequences grow more distant, as
here and there adjustments are made and grievances removed, the content of men's minds will
change. Political resentments may last long, but
in their nature they tend to diminish unless
special causes revive them. The normal concern,
after all, of most men in all countries is how to
earn the necessities of life, or to add luxuries to
the necessities. Some men at all times, and most
men at some times, are more concerned with
political aspirations or ambitions or resentments.

But these are exceptional persons and exceptional periods. If the preventive machinery, aided by war memories and war weariness, can prevent the present political resentments from causing another war for a substantial time, the specifically political forces which make for danger should tend to diminish.

No similar tendency is to be expected as regards economic dangers.

In any future that we can foresee the main occupation and concern of mankind will be the economic struggle; competition between individuals and between groups, whether of the same or different countries, will remain a basic element in human life. The forces so engendered are potentially the strongest in the world, and if they are so developed and directed that their collective might comes in conflict with any human institution, it is difficult to conceive the institution that can withstand the strain.

For these reasons it is perhaps not too much to say that, on any reasonably long view of the future, the preventive machinery against war is likely to prevent purely political causes from leading to war unless they are reinforced by economic conflicts of interest and policy; but that, if the normal economic competition leads to methods and policies which create a growing sense of injury and injustice; if such methods and policies are identified with the collective authority of national Governments; if they supplement, strengthen and inflame political resentments, no preventive machinery is likely to withstand the strain indefinitely.

The Form taken by Economic Dangers to Peace under Modern Conditions

We have seen the probable importance of the economic factor in future dangers to peace. It is no less necessary to recognise the form which it is likely to take under modern conditions.

Economic causes have always been among those which have led to war. But the form they have assumed has been very different at different periods of history. In early ages we have the mass invasions of nomadic races. As national Governments developed, wars have been the normal methods by which their territory has been determined, and whether by extension of frontiers or acquisition of colonies wars have been a principal determinant in the distribution of races and their comparative prosperity. In many periods the forcible acquisition of neighbours' territories has been undertaken for mixed motives of power, glory, and the exploitation of new economic resources. As late as the nineteenth century we have the partition of Africa by a process of competitive diplomacy involving danger at every step, and the similarly competitive demarcation of spheres of influence, under predominantly economic motives, of such countries as China or Persia.

None of these forms of economic competition or conflict is characteristic of the present age. Some of them may, of course, recur, but for the time the form and direction are different. The fundamental new factor is the enormously increased expense and economic waste of war under modern conditions. No country is likely to engage in war against another which has the resources of an industrial civilisation solely in order to obtain economic benefits. Many wars in the past have given results to the victors which seemed to them more than commensurate with the cost and loss; many more have seemed likely to do so when they were undertaken. In the future this is impossible. It is even likely (though by no means so certain) that countries will refrain from the kind of bluffing diplomacy which attempts to wrest economic advantages or new territory at the recognised risk of war though without the desire to embark upon it. And there are other reasons too. The forcible domination of one civilised country by another is recognised as impracticable; the partitioning of the uncivilised parts of the world is more or less complete; and though the forcible transfer of colonies from one colonial power to another is not to be excluded from the possibilities of the future, the preventive machinery against war and the immense risks and cost involved make it unlikely that it will be undertaken as a sole and deliberate object of policy.

The characteristic form of the present and probable economic conflicts is not to be found in attempts to acquire new territory. *It is to be found in the use of the power of government to deflect the course of trade between one country or another.*

One consequence follows from the fact that this is now the characteristic form which the economic factor assumes in relation to the problem of maintaining peace. By comparison

with earlier economic policies it is likely to be
less obviously and directly related to the actual
occasion of war. If, in the past, a country desired
to acquire a rich contiguous territory or distant
colony it might obviously, and even openly, embark upon a war for the purpose, though even
then motives were often confused and other pre-
texts were invented. But a country is now unlikely to initiate war solely and deliberately
either to impose a measure of commercial policy
or to protest against one imposed by another.
The process is different. One provocative measure
is followed by retaliatory measures in return.
Intense national feeling is aroused. Those who
wish for other reasons to increase competitive
armaments find a national mood which helps
them in their object. All political antagonisms
are inflamed. The sense of fear and insecurity,
as similar measures are taken in the opposing
country, grows. And finally, perhaps on some
trivial occasion at the last, some form of hostile
action is taken. And when the League intervenes
its task is made more difficult, and may be made
impossible, by the long developing and deeply
rooted feelings of antagonism and injustice resulting from the economic action to which we
have referred.

What we have to do, therefore, in examining
in more detail economic problems is not to take
only those which are likely to be the actual
occasions of war, or even the direct and obvious
causes, but all those which to a serious extent
poison international relations and create international friction.

THE PART PLAYED BY GOVERNMENTS IN ECONOMIC COMPETITION

It is time now to consider in some detail the principal classes of cases in which Governments intervene or may intervene in economic competition, and so cause the dangers to international relations described above.

For this purpose it will be convenient to adopt the following classification, though some of the divisions necessarily overlap to some extent:

(1) Commercial Policy;
(2) Population Problems;
(3) Credit, Currency and Capital Problems;
(4) Transportation Problems;
(5) Raw Material Problems;
(6) Diplomacy in Relation to Competition;
(7) Internal Social Trouble and its Political Reactions.

A few comments will be made on questions that seem to be of particular interest under each of these headings. No full treatment is, however, possible even in outline in the space now at our disposal. For a further analysis the reader is referred to the Joint and Separate Memoranda by Professors Moritz Bonn and André Siegfried, prepared at the request of the League of Nations in April 1929, and printed under the heading, "Economic Tendencies Affecting the Peace of the World". No attempt will now be made to lay down anything like a doctrine or to preach solutions of the different problems raised. The object is rather to suggest questions for which special attention is desirable.

(1) *Commercial Policy*

As a sub-division of this class it is natural to think first of tariffs. For of all forms of Government action which affect the economic interests of other countries tariffs have the most extensive and considerable economic consequences. Nearly all countries have some protective tariffs, though they vary very greatly in range and in height; most countries depend to a substantial extent on both exports and imports. Most manufactured articles are subject to a duty as they pass the frontier; and the natural effect of duties is both to reduce imports and exports and to increase the price of the articles on which they are imposed. In these conditions no other measures of commercial policy, whether by way of subsidy or prohibition, have a comparable importance with tariffs in the general economy of the world. That is, however, the economic point of view. We are now concerned with the quite different point of view of what it is that is most important from the point of view of international relations; and it does not at all follow that because tariffs are economically most important they must be or will be the most dangerous source of conflicts and ill-will. It is true, of course, that as the natural range of economic activity grows wider while tariff units show no similar tendency to grow in size, the clash and conflict between the claims of nationalism and of economic interest increase, and tariffs more and more cramp industrial development and deflect the natural courses of channels of trade. But tariffs in themselves, even high tariffs, while economically important, will not necessarily have correspondingly serious political consequences on international relations. If tariffs, even high ones, are non-differential or differential only on accepted principles and conditions, are not very unequal and are reasonably stable, they are in all their effects very much like natural obstacles, mountain ranges, etc., which make transport more difficult or expensive; they involve some economic loss, but it is a measurable one; the economic organisation accepts them as a factor and adjusts itself, and the ill-feeling engendered may not be very great. Countries do not normally regard themselves as having a natural right to free entry into each other's markets. It is very different, however, if they are deprived, especially suddenly, of a right previously enjoyed for a long period; if large and important industries which have grown up in response to a trade demand made possible by free entry or low tariffs are suddenly dislocated or destroyed by new duties.

This is to say, that from our present point of view of the peace of the world and international goodwill, it is not so much tariffs as the arbitrary methods by which they are framed, imposed and changed that are a serious element in international relations. From this point of view, therefore, it may be well to concentrate attention rather on tariff-making methods than on the general issue of Free Trade or Protection. Free Trade may be preferable in the interests of general world prosperity, and if it could be secured might also involve the removal of many serious dangers to international relations. But in existing circumstances we may secure a larger return by concentrating upon a more immediately practicable goal than that of abolishing tariffs. What we most need is to reform their abuses.

There is enough to do even within this restricted sphere. Many countries still frame their tariffs under the pressure of organised interests with little consideration of the kind of dislocation that may be caused elsewhere, the only restraining influence—and that partial and ineffective—being the fear of retaliation. We have, however, enough in existing practice and recent policy to indicate the line of advance. Commercial treaties which have been renewed in the last few years in Europe give at least some temporary stability between the contracting States. They are, however, subject usually to denunciation within a short period. There have recently been negotiations for the purpose of making these agreements more stable, and, in particular, providing that changes should only be made after notice has been given and an opportunity of consultation afforded with any seriously affected State. These principles—a recognition of the desirability of greater stability and the legitimate interest of other countries in the imposition of new tariffs and of a right of prior consultation—might, if given a sufficient extension, make tariffs in time an immensely less serious source of friction in international relations.

In contrast with tariffs, State-aided dumping causes an amount of friction out of proportion to its economic effect. From time to time in a serious depression of some industry which can exert political pressure, a State assists its own nationals to sell for export at less than the home price. In these cases intense feeling is inevitably caused, and the effect on the general relations of the country resorting to this measure with other countries that both produce and import the commodity is at once noticeable. It is the combination of State association and dumping that is serious. A State subsidy to an industry, even an exporting industry, while resented, causes very much less resentment if it is not accompanied by dumping, that is, sold abroad at less than the home price. On the other hand, dumping, if not aided by the State, is restricted both in extent and in time by the pressure of home competition which is always tending to force down home prices to within the small margin of the cost of production; and in any case such resentment as is felt is confined to the private individuals who resort to it. The responsibility of nations is not involved.

(2) *Population Problems*

A whole group of problems centre round surplus population, emigration and immigration. We must not mistake the nature of these questions. There is no surplus of world population, nor any likelihood of one in any near future. There are still large areas of the world whose development is in its infancy. A world surplus may indeed come in time, but in no case soon, and many factors may postpone or prevent it. Birth rates may decrease from natural causes or deliberate control. For the present, and for long to come, we have only the problem of local surpluses in a world which, with the aid of modern science, can support much more than its total population.

And these local surpluses, it must be remembered, are surplus only in relation to a given world economic system and a given ability of the countries in question to pay for imports from elsewhere by selling exports. While we still, therefore, have a difficult enough problem, it is not in its nature insoluble. It should be possible, by national and international arrangements, to prevent these local surpluses driving the world to war.

But if explosions are to be prevented, the peoples of the world must work positively and co-operatively at finding a safety-valve for the explosive forces, and not merely defensively at national policies designed to direct the explosion elsewhere. And the formation of a world opinion on a few general principles would be a great assistance. Does the possession of an apparently surplus, and increasing, population give any kind of moral right to a country to aim at an extension of its territory, or alternatively for emigration of its nationals to other countries, or to greater freedom for its trade? Or should such a country be expected to adjust its population or its standard of living to its existing resources? Should the admitted and natural right of a country to limit immigration at least enough to retain its own racial integrity be regarded as subject to qualification if it cannot, with its existing population, develop its own territory, or can develop it only very slowly: and especially if some of its territory is for climatic reasons uninhabitable by its own nationals while suitable for those of another race? Along which of these principles, or by what combination of them, should the world

c

try to solve the problem of local surpluses? Ultimately the peace of the world may depend upon the answer to these questions.

(3) *Credit, Currency and Capital Problems*

The most important problems, under this category, perhaps centre round foreign loans to Governments and their collection. Action against a defaulting State in the interests of bondholders was an important factor in the history of the last century. The principles of policy, and a standard of recognised practice, urgently need working out. It would be unsuitable to attempt to set out a code of principles here. One comment may, however, be permitted. Two kinds of loan are relatively without danger to international relations. The first is that which remains throughout a private affair, with no Government support, the private banker and lender taking their own risk, charging a corresponding rate, relying upon the borrowing country's interest in maintaining its credit for future loans as the only "sanction", and standing the loss if default occurs. The second is that in which, governmental association being foreseen as inevitable, the requisite precautions, both as to the conditions of the loan and as to international reactions, are taken from the beginning. An example of the latter is the League scheme for Austria, where all the Governments likely to be concerned in success or failure carefully examined and agreed upon the conditions and use of the loan before it was issued. In contrast with these, the most dangerous form of loan is that which is regarded at first as a purely private transaction, negotiated by private per-

sons with the borrowing Government, without
regard to political considerations, but which
afterwards, when default occurs, proves to involve such interests as to result in governmental
action. Consider, for example, a large loan raised
by the unconstitutional monarch of a primitive
people for expenditure on personal luxuries, but
secured on the revenues of his country, and so
subscribed that the bondholders are ultimately
able to use the forces of their respective countries
to exact payment. The result is unjust to the tax-
payers alike of the borrowing and the lending
countries, and the measures of enforcement are
extremely likely to involve international complications.

(4) *Transportation Problems*

Most of the questions that come under this
heading arise from the fact that many countries
require to obtain their supplies, or despatch the
goods they sell, across intervening territory.
Happily the principle of "free transit" has a very
wide recognition, but the difficulty of giving
security against all possible interruption is
greater.

It is to the same general category that we must
assign the famous controversy as to the "freedom
of the seas", which raises issues too complicated
for discussion here.

(5) *Raw Material Problems*

Some great powers have occupied uncivilised
areas rich in natural resources. The actual process
of competitive occupation occasioned much friction and many conflicts. This process perhaps

passed its most dangerous phase with the partition of Africa in the nineteenth century. But the danger of conflicts over raw materials, though changed in form, still remains. Many countries, either in their domestic territories or their empire, possess a disproportionate share of the resources which are the raw materials of the industry of the whole world. How far this threatens future conflict obviously depends very greatly upon the policy which governs their sale. If the raw materials are available on equal terms to the whole world, the sovereignty over the territory in which they are produced is obviously of much less importance to international relations than if it were used to give a competitive advantage to the industry of a particular country. Dangers from this source are not imminent at present, because more, and not less, materials of practically every kind are being produced than industry needs; and because, largely for this reason, competition in their sale secures equal and easy conditions for all importing countries. It follows that this is a specially favourable period in which to try to secure agreement as to the principles which should permanently govern the supply of raw materials to other countries than those which need them. For it is much easier to prevent, than to terminate, provocative and preferential practices.

(6) *Diplomacy in Relation to Competition*

A little recognised, but important, source of friction in international relations arises from the use of the diplomatic machine to assist nationals in economic competition. This is especially notice-

able in the case of the legations of great Powers
operating in the capitals of small countries. A
large part of the current daily work of such legations consists, in fact, of helping their respective
nationals to obtain contracts and concessions.
How far is it right and desirable that a Minister,
or a commercial attaché, acting under his responsibility, should go in work of this kind?
There is a singular absence of any recognised
etiquette limiting the sphere and prescribing the
methods permissible to those who, as official representatives, necessarily engage the collective
responsibility of their respective countries in anything they do. Clearly it is right that they should
insist on justice and fair treatment. It may also
be convenient that they should supply information as to local law and custom, and perhaps
trade opportunities, though trade organisations
organised privately might do work of this kind.
But unhappily a Minister often goes much further than this. He represents it as a matter of
some interest to his Government that a contract
or a concession or a loan issue should be given to
a firm of his own nationality. His representation
may carry suggestions as to political favour or
displeasure; and if negotiations of quite a different
character, such as the arrangement of an Entente
or Alliance, or the funding of a foreign debt, are
in progress between the two countries, the minis-
terial intervention may well be decisive. Is a
Minister justified in using pressure of this kind?
Certainly when a Minister is suspected of doing
so by others, resentment follows, and the disturbance in the relations between the legations is
transmitted to their respective Foreign Offices. In

the meantime the impact of such competitive business diplomacy upon the politics of small European capitals is often very regrettable. Here again the point to retain is that practice, in fact, varies considerably; different Ministers and countries have differing standards. There is no generally recognised and observed code of behaviour in such matters, and in its absence friction is inevitable. This may seem to many a trivial source of economic difficulties, but not to those who have watched closely the working of legations in small capitals.

(7) *Internal Social Trouble and its Political Reactions*

Little need be said under this heading, as it is covered by other papers.[1] For the sake of completeness, however, it must be noted that there are a number of countries in which grave social trouble, or revolution, if it occurred, would be likely to lead to international complications and perhaps foreign intervention.

We have now reviewed, necessarily in bare outline, the main forms which economic dangers are likely to assume. The questions which arise are set out in much greater detail in the Bonn-Siegfried Memoranda already referred to.

As we have seen, the characteristic form of the economic danger, in modern conditions, arises from the use of the instrument of government to influence economic competition, and the absence of any adequate code of recognised behaviour.

[1] See Supplementary Reports, pp. 185-231.

Preventive and Remedial Action

The fundamental question remains as to what preventive and remedial action can be taken, and, in particular, what contribution different classes of the world community can make to that action.

It will have emerged from what has been said that what is most needed is effective world agreement as to the principles which should guide Governments in the action they take affecting the economic interests of other countries, and therefore international relations.

Now, in some cases it may be that such principles can in the near future be directly negotiated between Governments and embodied in conventions. It is quite possible, for example, that a valuable convention may be obtained regarding the "treatment of foreigners" who are admitted to residence in each country, and securing for them in general equal treatment as regards business facilities, taxation, etc. We can also contemplate treaties being made to cover some part of the tariff problem, to provide, for example, for some prior consultation before new tariffs are imposed which would disastrously affect foreign industries.

It is clear, however, that, over the greater range of the problems we have discussed, the time is not ripe for effective governmental negotiations. In many cases such negotiations would either fail or, even worse, would consolidate practices and customs involving danger to future international relations. In these cases before discussion can usefully proceed between the representatives of Governments, preliminary re-

search and study, unofficial and public discussion,
and the gradual building up of a body of informed
and interested world public opinion are essential.
For this purpose the active interest, on the one
hand, of universities, and centres of teaching and
learning of every kind, and on the other, of all
institutions which organise and direct informed
discussion of matters affecting international relations, needs to be enlisted.

And for a movement for inquiries, discussion,
and world public education of this kind, the great
institutions which guide and represent the religious forces of the world can supply a motive
power and force of inestimable value and decisive
effect.

No better conclusion can be found for this
report than the solemn words of M. Theunis, the
President of the World Economic Conference of
1927—the most authoritative conference that
has ever met to discuss the world's economic
problems.

The Conference, M. Theunis pointed out, had
passed a resolution stating the "unanimous conviction that the maintenance of world peace
depends largely upon the principles on which the
economic policies of nations are formed and exe-
cuted; that the Governments and peoples of all
countries should constantly take counsel together as to this aspect of the economic problem;
and that we should look forward to the establishment of a recognised body of principles designed
to eliminate the economic difficulties which cause
friction and misunderstanding. Economic conflicts", he continued, "and divergence of eco-

nomic interest are perhaps the most serious and
the most permanent of all the dangers which are
likely to threaten the peace of the world. No
machinery for the settlement of international
disputes can be relied upon to maintain peace if
the economic policies of the world so develop as
to create not only deep divergences of economic
interest between different masses of the world's
population but a sense of intolerable injury and
injustice. No task is more urgent or more vital
than that of securing agreement on certain principles of policy which are necessary in the
interests of future peace."

[Detailed studies of the subjects of Raw Materials,
Tariffs, and Migration, prepared by Professors Jacob
Viner, André Siegfried, and Moritz Bonn respectively,
will be found in the Supplementary Section of this Vol.]

II

INDUSTRIAL AND LABOUR INFLUENCES

By G. A. JOHNSTON

1. INTRODUCTION

INFLUENCES in the industrial and labour field are often more truly the underlying causes of war than the events which constitute the actual occasions for the declaration of war. The immediate occasions of war are various, and often trivial; for example, the rash act of some commander of troops or warships, the alteration of a telegram by some diplomatist, the assassination of some official personage, and so on. It is a commonplace that these occasions are not the real causes of war. The real, as contrasted with the ostensible, causes are not often clear. It is probable that no great war was ever due to a single cause. Wars are rather the result of a group of causes, the most apparent of which are not always the most fundamental. The fundamental causes of war are usually to be found in the slow development of tendencies and policies which may begin to develop for years, and even for generations, before the actual explosion takes place. The development of some of these influences is so gradual that it is only when comparison is made over considerable periods that it is possible to be sure that movement has taken place at all. It is necessary to be clear on this point, because the influences that make for war in the industrial and labour sphere are usually to be found in the background and are rarely, if ever, explicitly recognised among the causes of war.

This report deals with the influences which make for war in the widest sense of the word "war". It will refer not only to wars between nations, but also to civil wars. It will include in the influences that make for war those which have led to revolts, rebellions, and revolutions. For all these manifestations are of the essential nature of war and employ the appropriate methods of war.

It is not generally recognised that there are labour and industrial influences making for war. There is, indeed, universal agreement that the economic causes of war are numerous and important; but economic causes are generally interpreted to refer to commerical and financial elements rather than to factors in the field of labour and industry. The tendency to overlook the industrial and labour influences making for war can be illustrated from a brief survey of some classifications of the causes of war that have actually been given.

Some forty different causes of war were enumerated by the speakers at the Conference on the Cause and Cure of War called at Washington in 1925 by nine national women's organisations of the United States. These causes were classified in four main catgories: psychological, economic, political, and social. Only three of the forty causes thus classified refer even indirectly to the sphere of industry and labour; they are "migration barriers", "social inequalities", and "economic rivalries".

Another classification of the causes or sources of war, which mentions forty-one different sources, is published by Mr. Tell A. Turner in his *Causes of War and the New Revolution.*[1] In this book Mr. Turner passes in review all the most important wars since 1588, and carefully analyses their causes. Mr. Turner classifies his forty-one sources of war in five main categories: economic, dynastic, nationalistic, religious, and sentimental, only two of which would appear to refer to industrial influences, namely, "quarrels over industries" and "mines".

Three other classifications of the causes of war may be mentioned. Professor A. C. Pigou maintains that, in the last analysis, the real fundamental causes of war are two in number: the desire for domination, and the desire for gain.[2] Of these two fundamental causes the desire for gain is, of course, primarily economic, and directly involves various forms of industrial influence. The desire for domination may also involve economic considerations. The economist naturally emphasises the economic causes of war.

A careful examination of modern wars from the point of view of their causality, made by Mr.

[1] Tell A. Turner, *Causes of War and the New Revolution*, Boston, 1927, p. 174.
[2] *The Political Economy of War*, London, 1921, p. 16.

John Bakeless,[1] yields the result, to his mind, that the larger proportion of these wars had economic causes. Mr. Bakeless maintains that of the twenty principal wars between 1878 and 1918 sixteen have had self-evident economic causes. These causes are to be found in colonial rivalries, tariff discrimination, and efforts to secure raw materials. Mr. Bakeless points out that frequently the underlying cause of hostilities does not appear directly, and the war would appear to be solely the result of non-economic factors, until the immediate cause, upon further examination, is seen to be the outcome of trade rivalry or the desire to protect economically important colonies, and to be thus in its essence economic.

A much older classification than either that has yet been given also recognises the place of economic causes of war. In 1866 Lecky classified wars under three headings: "Wars produced by opposition of religious belief, wars resulting from erroneous economical notions, either concerning the balance of trade or the material advantages of conquest, and wars resulting from the collision of the two hostile doctrines of the Divine right of kings and the rights of nations".[2]

While, however, as we have seen, all these classifications give a prominent place to economic causes, few, if any, of them explicitly recognise influences in the industrial and labour field. Our question, therefore, is: In spite of the tendency to ignore industrial and labour influences making for war, do such influences really exist and operate?

[1] *The Economic Causes of Modern War*, New York, 1921.
[2] Lecky, *Rationalism in Europe*, London, 1866, vol. ii. p. 219.

The fact that industrial and labour conditions exercise an influence in respect of peace and war was explicitly recognised by the Treaty of Versailles. The Preamble of Part XIII of that Treaty contains the following phrase: "Whereas conditions of labour exist involving such injustice, hardship, and privation to large numbers of people as to produce unrest so great that the peace and harmony of the world are imperilled..." The Preamble further states that universal peace can be established only if it is based on social justice. The implications of this declaration will engage us in detail later. At the moment it is sufficient to note the fundamental implication, which is that all influences inimical to the realisation of social justice are influences dangerous to the maintenance of peace.

2. HISTORICAL INSTANCES OF INDUSTRIAL AND LABOUR CAUSES OF WAR

A careful reading of history shows that the declaration contained in the Peace Treaty is not an *a priori* philosophical proposition, but is founded on the experience of the ages. Industrial and labour causes have frequently brought unrest so great as to lead to rebellion and to war. Where hardship and privation exist there is a fruitful cause of the conflicts of war. Modern war is not essentially different from the brigandage of the Homeric chieftains and the state piracy of Polycrates. War as Aristotle described it is a "means of acquisition" and "a species of hunting". Individuals who have been bargaining against foreigners in the market-place adjourn as soldiers to the battle-field to continue the debate. Whether this takes place in the simple conditions of a Greek City State or in the infinitely more complex field of modern international economy, the predisposing cause is often "hardship and privation".

It would not be difficult to prepare a catalogue of wars in which industrial and labour influences have constituted one at least of the underlying causes. It will be sufficient to mention three illustrative instances. In England, the Peasants' Revolt of 1381, one of the most spontaneous rebellions that ever took place in England, was directly due to the hardships and privations of the peasants and artisans, resulting from the long succession of legislative measures, beginning with the Statute of Labourers, 1351, intended to deal with the labour situation produced by the ravages of the Black Death. This instance is significant as an indication of the slowness with which influences in the labour and industrial field sometimes make themselves felt. This great epidemic took place in 1348 to 1349. About one-third of the population died, and by a necessary economic law there was immediately a tendency for wages to rise. The legislative efforts made to prevent this rise were only partially successful, but they brought about such hardship and privation as to lead to the gradual growth of unrest so great as to goad the peasants into open revolt, but not until 1381, or more than thirty years after.

The Thirty Years' War, 1618 to 1648, although due to a variety of causes—religious, dynastic and others—was perhaps fundamentally the resultant of the restlessness of the peoples of Central

Europe, induced by bad conditions of labour and hardships due to oppression.

Nor can it be seriously doubted that one of the underlying causes of the French Revolution and the wars which were its immediate sequel, complex as they are, is ultimately to be found in social unrest arising from circumstances affecting labour, as they had been developing for generations. The force of the Revolution came from the sudden liberation of the peasants from their feudal dues and local tyrannies after the autumn of 1789.

One of the clearest cases of war resulting, in part at least, from labour and industrial causes is the American Civil War. Much as views differ as to the precise causality of that war, there is general agreement that its ultimate cause was to be found in the question of slavery. No doubt the South fought for disruption and the North for the preservation of the Union of the States, but the consequent struggle would not have taken place had it not been for the issue of slavery. Slave labour was productive of great profits to the South: it meant little or nothing economically to the North. The South, intimately in contact with the everyday operation of the system, defended it on legal, economic, and also on moral grounds. Ultimately the question was one definitely in the field of labour and industry.

It would be easy to multiply the instances which have been given. They have been chosen because each is to be found in the areas of what have now become the four greatest industrial countries.

3. ANALYSIS AND CLASSIFICATION OF INDUSTRIAL AND LABOUR INFLUENCES MAKING FOR WAR

The analysis of the precise conditions of labour and industry constituting the influences which may lead to war will be facilitated if it is recognised that, under the conditions of the modern world, one of the most important predisposing influences leading to war is the pressure of population. When a country is aware that the pressure of population is becoming too great to be supported in accordance with previously applied methods of utilising its resources, it has so far found in general two, and only two, solutions to this problem. One is emigration, the other is intensive industrialisation. By a curious fatality, action in accordance with either one or the other of these solutions is apt to bring the State into conflict with other Powers. If the solution of emigration is chosen, such emigration may take place in two or three different ways. In the first place, in order to find land for its emigrants, the State may colonise, and colonisation is apt to lead to war either with other colonising Powers or with the natives whom the new settlers displace. In other cases migration may take place into the territories of other sovereign States. In such cases, the country of emigration is rarely willing that those who have left it should become completely absorbed in the population of the new country and lose all contact with their motherland. There is a tendency for the State of emigration to encourage its emigrants to retain their original nationality, to continue to perform

D

military service, to retain their language, and in other ways to remain, even in the country of immigration, a detached unit of the population of the motherland. The tendency of the State of immigration is naturally and equally obviously in conflict with the policy of the motherland. No State of immigration likes to contemplate the continuance of essentially foreign-minded groups and communities within its borders, owing allegiance to another State. Its policy is to absorb as rapidly and completely as possible the various heterogeneous elements and to weld them into one homogeneous whole. Such conflict of policy and practice is obviously an influence which may make for war.

The other main solution open to the country which is feeling the pressure of population is industrialisation. As population grows, the capacity of the country to supply food for this growing population becomes less and less adequate. The State has to look beyond its own borders for food for its population. In order to pay for this food it must export manufactured articles. In order to export manufactured articles it must manufacture them. To do this it often requires to import raw materials, and it is essential for it to search actively for markets for its wares. The development of foreign trade involves international relations which may not be free from the conditions of conflict.

An illustration of the dilemma in which a country with a growing pressure of population finds itself may be supplied in the case of Japan. Japan, faced in the last fifty years with a rapidly growing population, a population already press-

ing hard upon the food-producing capacity of the
country, found itself obliged to choose between
the policies of emigration and industrialisation.
It did not choose the policy of emigration, for
several reasons. One reason is the fundamental
dislike of the Japanese to migrate. Even when
no restrictions were imposed by other Powers on
Japanese immigration, comparatively few Japanese left their own shores. At the present time
only some 350,000 Japanese are to be found outside the Japanese Empire, China, and Siberia.
The second reason why Japan has not chosen the
policy of emigration is that very few actual
possibilities of emigration were open to the
Japanese. It has been said, and with some truth,
that migration of labour is always from the
low-standard to the high-standard country. The
operation of this principle has, in fact, prevented
the emigration of the Japanese to China, to
Korea, and to Manchuria. On the other hand, the
high-standard countries, such as the United
States, Canada, Australia, and New Zealand, have
imposed, either by law or in practice, restrictions on the free movement of Japanese into
their countries. For all these reasons Japan,
being unable to adopt the solution of emigration
for its problem of the pressure of population,
definitely decided to adopt the solution of industrialisation. Japan has deliberately embarked
on a policy of industrial expansion with a view
to supplying not only its own needs in manufactured articles, but also to becoming one of the
world's great exporting countries. The value of
the production of the manufacturing industries
of Japan increased more than five-fold between

1914 and 1926. In order to make this industrial development possible, Japan has naturally required to seek raw materials and markets. This search has already involved it in serious differences of opinion with China. China, including Manchuria, is the obvious market for Japanese goods, and Manchuria is an immensely valuable source of its raw materials. The problem of Manchuria, which is regarded in Pacific countries as the most dangerous part of the world's surface from the point of view of the possibility of future war, is essentially connected with the necessity of the development of industrialism in Japan.

The influences in the sphere of industry and labour making for war may be classified in three categories: first, those resulting from the nature of the industrial order; second, those resulting from lack of balance between production and consumption; and finally, those resulting from bad conditions of work. Though the lines of demarcation between these three kinds of influences may not in all cases be absolutely theoretically clear, it would appear desirable for the practical purposes of this report to apply this threefold classification.

4. INFLUENCES DUE TO THE NATURE OF THE INDUSTRIAL ORDER

The extent to which industrialisation may constitute an influence making for war will become clear if we analyse the meaning of industrialisation. The industrial order is the system under which commodities are produced by labour specialised and organised to operate machinery on a large scale. This definition directly implies all the chief characteristics of that order. In the first place, it is the system of large-scale machine production with standardisation of product. In the second place, it implies organisation of labour, the regimentation of work-people under discipline. Thirdly, this work must be specialised; division of labour and specialisation of function are involved. In the fourth place, industrialism involves centralisation of factories and consequently of population. Finally, it involves capitalisation.

Of these characteristics, those which are of most interest for our study are the first, second, and third. One of the other characteristics, with which we shall not deal, namely, capitalisation, is of great importance from the standpoint of war and peace. This point is not dealt with here because it would appear to belong more particularly to the section of the report dealing with the economic and financial influences that make for war.

What is the influence on peace and war of machine production or the mechanisation of industry? Experience shows that in the development of the use of machinery in manufacture a general principle has been at work. This principle may be formulated in various ways, but no better expression can be given to it than that of Marshall: "Any manufacturing operation that can be reduced to uniformity so that exactly the same thing has to be done over and over again in the same way is sure to be taken over sooner or later by machinery." It may be difficult to invent the necessary machinery, delays and obstacles may have to be overcome, but if the work to which machinery is to be applied is on a sufficiently large scale, it is certain that sooner or later the operation will be handed over to the machine.

But machinery will only be invented and will only be used if the products to be manufactured are susceptible of standardisation and if there is sufficient demand for them to make it possible to produce them on a large scale. If the demand for a certain article is small, and is not susceptible of expansion, then machinery will not be used in its manufacture. Similarly, if uniform, standardised products are not desired, then again machinery will not be used, because it is a characteristic of the machine to turn out each article and each part exactly similar to the last. Machine production, then, is essentially large-scale production, and is essentially the production of standardised articles.

It has frequently been maintained that machine production or mechanisation, as explained above, has a destructive effect on human society. Mr. R. Austin Freeman, for example, has said: "Mechanism, by its reactions on man and his environment, is antagonistic to human welfare. . . . It has destroyed social unity and replaced it by social disintegration and class antagonism to an extent which directly threatens civilisation . . . and finally, by its reactions on the activities of war, it constitutes an agent for the wholesale destruction of man and his works . . ." Similar indictments have so frequently been made that it is necessary to consider briefly their foundation.

It cannot, of course, be doubted that mechan-

isation has, from the economic standpoint, many
advantages. It has undoubtedly led to the production of a greater sum of material wealth
throughout the world. The main causes leading
to this have been the increased efficiency and
absence of waste due to the large-scale employment of machinery. It is characteristic of machine
production to utilise to the fullest extent products
which in an earlier state of society were regarded
as mere waste. The utilisation of machinery, in
addition to avoiding waste, has led to a great
improvement in the efficiency of labour. It is a
commonplace that thanks to machinery a single
workman now produces many times as much as
he is able to do without machinery.

But, it may be objected, if it is admitted that
the material basis of the welfare of the community is improved as a result of mechanisation,
what of the individual producers themselves, the
workers whose functions are largely reduced to
those of machine tenders? What has been the
repercussion on their lives of machine production? Has the personality of the worker not
suffered? Is there not a risk that he should become a mere appendage to the machine?

The most important consideration in this connection is that machine production inevitably
involves a certain degree of monotony since it
involves much mere repetition. Even if it be
admitted that monotony is not felt to result from
the actual repetitive process so much as from
the general atmosphere of the factory, and even
if it be further agreed that monotony is not an
objective quality of things but a subjective feeling of persons, it must be maintained that the

monotony involved in the constitution of the industrial order has real importance from the standpoint of peace and war. For if work is merely repetitive and requires no concentrated effort of attention on the part of the operative, his mind necessarily falls into a state of reverie and he is apt to become a prey to various complexes, one of the most common of which is persecution mania. His mind, not engrossed in his work because there is nothing in his work to engross it, becomes obsessed with the small worries and injustices inevitably involved in the routine of life. Constantly revolving these small difficulties in his mind, the worker becomes more and more discontented and is apt to develop into an unstable and unprofitable member of society.

And a further consideration is involved. The needs of human welfare necessarily require a certain degree of change and variety in life. If change and variety are completely absent from the conditions of the working day, they are necessarily sought, and rightly sought, after working hours. If, however, reverie during working hours has introduced a state of mind of discontent and unrest, the change that is sought after working hours may involve violent, subversive, and revolutionary strains of thought and of action.

The regimentation of labour under conditions of organisation and discipline has such an important bearing on questions of peace and war that it is necessary to emphasise its implications. The industrial order would not be possible, however much machinery existed, if work-people could not be obtained to tend the machines, willing to submit to employment for regular hours in premises supplied by the employer, and under a certain amount of discipline. The organisation of the workers under conditions involving discipline is, in fact, a necessary consequence of the application of machinery in industry. In the industrial order, the employer supplies the machinery and the premises in which it is situated. He naturally wishes to reduce to the minimum such overhead charges as the provision of power to the machines, lighting, and heating. It is essential, therefore, from the standpoint of economy of production, that under normal circumstances his work-people should begin work at the same time and finish work at the same time. And regularity of work has another *raison d'être*. The factory worker, as in a rolling mill, for instance, or a shipbuilding yard, frequently forms one of a small group employed on a single operation or closely connected series of operations. If one member of the group is absent, the group as a whole is thrown idle. Regularity of work is therefore realised to be necessary not only in the interests of the employer, but frequently also directly in the interests of the workers themselves.

Under the factory system, work is not only regulated in its duration, but regulated also in its intensity. In an early stage of industrial development, a sufficient intensity of work is assured by means of foremen, one of whose chief functions is to stimulate the workers' regular and sustained effort. In a somewhat later stage, the same object is attained either by means of piece-work systems of wages, according to which the

worker has a direct monetary interest in increased
output, or by means of profit-sharing and co-
partnership systems, giving him an indirect
financial interest in increased production. In the
third stage of development, while the employer
may still rely practically on either or both of the
above means, his chief method of securing intense unremitting labour is to subordinate, in
cases where the conditions of manufacture make
this possible, the work of the worker to the auto-
matic rhythm of the machine.

If the necessity to submit to industrial discipline no longer, in general, produces serious
unrest among the workers in highly industrialised
countries, it is none the less true that this is
simply the consequence of long habituation. In
almost every country serious industrial unrest,
sometimes resulting in riot and rebellion, has
accompanied the first beginnings of the industrial
revolution. In countries now in process of industrialisation, such as China, the question of
factory discipline has given rise to more unrest
than any other single question in the industrial
field, and it is at the root of some of the bitterest
opposition on the part of China to foreign industrial operations.

Another influence for war or peace in connection with the nature of the industrial order
is the centralisation of factories, and consequently of population, which it involves. The
precise causes of the centralisation and localisation of industry vary greatly, and sometimes it
is only with difficulty that they can be discerned.
There are, however, four general types of cause

which may be broadly distinguished, namely: (1) availability of raw materials; (2) convenience to markets; (3) suitability of climatic and other conditions; and (4) accessibility to sources of power. By far the most important causes of localisation and centralisation of industry have been propinquity to power and convenience to markets. And this has meant, in the development of the industrial order, propinquity to coal-fields, for coal has been the chief source of cheap power, and accessibility to the sea, for the sea is the common highway which leads to all the markets of the world.

From the standpoint of war and peace, this conclusion is of the first importance. For some of the worst of the social effects of the industrial order have been due to the excessive overcrowding of the people in the cities of factories which have sprung up near coal-fields and at seaports. The people have been forced by the centralisation of industry to live in dingy tenements under skies perpetually obscured by curtains of smoke. Under these circumstances, the realisation of the genuine ends of peace has been impossible either in work or in leisure. A deep sense of social injustice has grown up in the serried ranks of the workers and has fertilised the seeds of revolution and war.

5. Influences Due to the Lack of Balance between Production and Consumption

The lack of balance between production and consumption manifested in the recurring trade cycles which have been so marked a feature of the industrial history of recent years, is of interest from the standpoint of peace and war in two, respects.

In the first place, it has given rise to the artificial stimulation of consumption, and in the second place, it has been directly responsible for the prevalence of unemployment.

Under modern industrial conditions, where mass-production involves the output of vast quantities of goods for which no consumer has yet asked, it is necessary for the producer, by means of elaborate systems of salesmanship and advertisement, to persuade the consumer to take his goods. In the pre-industrial era the consumer ordered the producer to produce an article for his consumption. Under modern industrial conditions the producer manufactures goods and induces the consumer to take them. This change in the relations of the producer and the consumer has inevitably meant that the producer has developed an amazingly efficient system of machinery for the marketing of his wares. He has done everything to stimulate consumption and to create new wants. Through advertisement the producer has stimulated the indeterminate wants of the people and has incited the buyer to decide in favour of satisfying one particular desire rather than another. Further, by means of the development of instalment selling and other methods of the same kind, the consumer is induced to buy what he is not yet in a position to pay for. Wants are stimulated to such an extent that their satisfaction outruns the existing resources of the consumer. The future is mortgaged to satisfy the stimulated, and in some cases artificially stimulated, needs of the present.

The artificial stimulation of consumption has an influence on questions of war and peace in two connections.

In the first place, within an individual country, as a result of the creation of new wants and the parading before the eyes of the people of the attractiveness of goods which they cannot purchase, discontent is widely aroused. This has been particularly notable in the countries of the East. Highly desirable goods are brought to the attention of people without the means of purchasing them. The inevitable result is discontent, running into debt in order to purchase goods which cannot be afforded, and, it may be, for the first time a real recognition of poverty. In many an Eastern village people have not recognised that they were poor until their needs and desires and wants were stimulated by the marketing of mass-produced goods. The question, of course, arises whether it is better for a man to be poor and not know it and to be contented, or to know that he is poor and be discontented. The discussion of this question would, however, lead us too far away from the subject of this report.

The second respect in which marketing and the stimulation of consumption has an influence from the standpoint of war and peace is in its international repercussions. The necessity of finding markets has impelled the producer not only to look for them in his own country but to cross frontiers and to find markets in other lands. This has necessarily led to the development of international trade, which has become particularly marked in recent years. The various manufacturing countries find themselves in competition for the raw materials of the world; they find themselves in competition also to supply the growing markets of the world. Everywhere competition is intensified to find raw materials in the cheapest markets, to sell manufactured goods in the dearest. A great network of trade has grown up which has covered the whole world and invaded and broken down the self-sufficiency of Indian and Chinese village communities, and even of the family unit of the South Sea Islands. Since the Great War, as the economic interdependence of the world has become more and more marked, international trade has led to keener and keener competition, involving on the one hand the establishment of international trusts and cartels and on the other the movement for the raising of tariffs. But the examination of the influence of these factors on questions of war and peace belongs more properly to the economic report.

The lack of balance between production and consumption, not only within individual countries, but in the world as a unit, is ultimately responsible for the prevalence of unemployment. No analysis of modern conditions making for war would be complete without some reference to unemployment. The worker who has been out of work for a long time necessarily tends to become demoralised, necessarily tends to question the conditions of society in which he lives. The wide extent of unemployment is one of the new characteristics of the modern industrial world. It has been called "the cancer of the body economic". It is to be found in every industrial country in the world and under every form of political and economic organisation. At the present moment, a conservative estimate of the total number of workers unemployed in the world would show not less than ten million unemployed. It may be assumed that each of these unemployed workers has two people dependent upon him or her, so that, at least, thirty[1] million men, women, and children are at any one moment suffering through unemployment.

One of the worst effects of unemployment, from the standpoint of its influence on the worker, is the demoralisation which it tends to produce. Significant expression is given to this aspect of the problem in a report of the Children's Bureau of the U.S. Department of Labor : "The most important feature of unemployment is its effect on the family morale—the father idle about the house, unsettled, disheartened; the mother going out to work if she can secure it, and using up every bit of her strength in the double task of providing for the family's maintenance and caring for the household and the children; the children suffering from the depression and uncertainty of what the future may mean."[2]

Another effect on the worker of long-continued unemployment is that the unemployed worker necessarily tends to develop a sentiment of solidarity with other unemployed. All the unemployed tend to constitute a solid section of the

[1] These figures (February 1932) are about sixteen and fifty millions respectively.—EDITOR.

[2] U.S. Dept. of Labor, Children's Bureau, *Unemployment and Child Welfare*, Washington, 1923.

community, a section in which all the evils of
mob psychology tend to develop. If in any
country a large number of men are unemployed
over long periods of time, these sentiments of
demoralisation and solidarity with the other
unemployed, embittered by the vision of the
sufferings of dependent women and children,
obviously bear within them the seeds of social
catastrophe.

6. Influences Due to Bad Conditions of Work

It is necessary now to consider a further series
of influences, namely, those resulting from bad
conditions of work.

Bad conditions of work are of importance from
the standpoint of war and peace because they
naturally produce discontent and dissatisfaction.
When the individual worker becomes fully conscious that his conditions of work are bad and
realises that he can do nothing through his own
individual initiative to produce an improvement
in them, his tendency in all industrial countries
has been to organise with other industrial workers
in trade unions. The trade union, through its collective initiative, attempts to secure an improvement in conditions of work for its members,
improvements which the members individually
cannot obtain. If methods of negotiation with the
employers fail to secure the improvements desired
by the organised workers, the method of the strike
is resorted to.

While the method of the strike and of the lock-
out has, as such, no essential relation to questions

of war and peace, strikes and lock-outs are none the less methods of conflict. The settlement of industrial disputes by means of strikes and lock-outs is akin to the settlement of political disputes by means of war.

There is, further, one of the developments of the strike which constitutes a direct analogy with war. The theory of the general strike, particularly as developed by French Syndicalist thinkers of the later nineteenth and earlier twentieth century, regarded the general strike as essentially directed to the overthrow of the existing order of society. The general strike was essentially a political weapon, governed by essentially warlike aims. The terminology of the Syndicalist theorists of the general strike is the terminology of war. The strike was to be an instrument of revolution and the means of leading to the world-wide conquest of the means of production by the proletariat.

It is clear that if a worker's conditions of life are so bad that under no circumstances does it seem to him that they can be worse, a particularly fruitful field is provided for the artificial stimulation of mass movements of revolution.

An important aspect of bad labour conditions, productive of conditions which may serve the ends of war, is unduly long hours of work. Long hours, producing undue fatigue, leaving no time for leisure, no inclination to read, no opportunity for reflection, render the worker particularly liable to fall an easy prey to propaganda. Ignorance and weariness are the best foundation on which those who wish to stimulate war and revolt can work. In this connection, the evil effects of long hours may be distinguished into two main

E

groups: (*a*) those that result from undue fatigue, and (*b*) those that follow from absence of leisure.

(*a*) It is clear that fatigue may be either physical, the result of a definite physiological condition of the muscles of the body, or else mental, manifesting itself in weariness, boredom, and inability for continued concentration. It is not to be expected that all fatigue can be eliminated by means of even the most scientifically arranged rest pauses. All that is usually done by the interpolation of rest pauses is to delay the onset of fatigue until the end of the working day. The problem of the diminution of fatigue, in the interests both of the worker and the employer, requires for its solution not only a study of the distribution of work and of rest pauses, but also of the total length of the working day and its relation to the period of rest before the work of the next day begins. Long continued fatigue, the results of which are not immediately apparent, produces feelings of unrest and dissatisfaction so serious as to imperil the stability of the social fabric.

(*b*) The absence of leisure leads to the arrest of mental development and prevents the growth of interests other than those connected directly with the work on which the workman is engaged. Now one great value of leisure, from the psychological standpoint, is that instincts and impulses which are baulked or suppressed during hours of work can find free expression during spare time. The rigid discipline of modern industry renders impossible during hours of work the expression of most of the instincts and impulses natural to man. It is only in leisure time that these in-

stincts can be given free play. Leisure enables
people to satisfy the universal desire for variety
and change, and the desire to play more than one
rôle in life.

Further, it is only in spare time that, under the
conditions of developed industrialism, work-
people have opportunity for the enjoyment and
exercise of the social activities of the family. A
striking instance of the way in which the enjoyment of family life is bound up with the question
of hours of work is contained in the report of the
Interchurch World Movement on the American
steel strike of 1919. According to that report, one
of the strikers against the 12-hour day in the
American Iron and Steel Industry gave as his
reason "the fact that his little daughter had died
within the last few months; he said that he had
never known the child because he was at work
when she was awake, or else he was asleep during
the day time. He was determined that he would
know the other children, and for that reason felt
that it was imperative that he should have the
8-hour day." Long hours of work, inimical to the
full development of family life, cannot be other
than an influence making for social instability.
That the good father of a family is the best citizen
has long been a commonplace of political thought.

It is in spare time, finally, that the work-people
have an opportunity for the exercise of civic
duties in their city and in their State. Unless they
have a reasonable amount of spare time, it is
impossible for them to discharge adequately and
conscientiously these duties of citizenship which
modern life has rendered more and more complex
and difficult.

Special kinds of labour, such as the forms of labour demanded or required of native workers in colonial countries, are also the material out of which war may arise. Forced labour, compulsory labour, stimulated labour, contract labour, all of these are alike in requiring from the worker discipline, in some cases under penal sanctions, and in a situation in which he necessarily feels himself un-free. Such conditions of labour, regarded as analogous to slavery, are the material out of which revolts have frequently sprung. When such forms of labour are employed on a large scale in private industrial or agricultural enterprises, the possibilities of explosion are obviously great. It was not the slaves in domestic employment in Athens, but those who worked in the silver mines of Laureion, who revolted. In modern history also instances are not lacking of rebellions and wars due to slavery or to forms of labour which, while the labourers are free, involve some of the restrictions of slavery.

Various other questions in the field of labour and industry, while not at first sight likely to involve international or social conflicts or disturbance, do in fact constitute influences making for international tension. For example, the question of the work of women during the night in factories has led to a considerable amount of tension in Asiatic countries. A country which permits the work of women at night in industrial undertakings, particularly in the textile industry —thus making possible the adoption of the three-shift system—would appear to be at an advantage from the point of view of international competition over a country which has abolished night work for women. A sense of social injustice, a sense of the absence of fair play, arises in these cases which may lead to bitterness and even to serious differences of opinion between countries. A further respect in which bad conditions of work may be considered to produce international friction arises from the fact that a country in which conditions of work are generally high may contain within its borders areas in which unsatisfactory conditions in certain departments, for example, child labour, are, for various reasons, allowed to continue to exist. Such local bad conditions are felt by the country concerned to be a kind of skeleton in the cupboard, reference to which in other countries may be considered to be likely to create unfriendly feeling.

Perhaps, however, the most important feature of bad conditions of work, from the standpoint of war and peace, is to be found in unduly low wages. Low wages, by depressing the standard of life and keeping the worker and his family in hardship and poverty, render him particularly liable to social revolution. The reason given for the majority of strikes in the principal industrial countries, and particularly in Great Britain and the United States, is the workers' desire for wages higher than the employers offer. The official statistics show that out of the aggregate number of work-people directly involved in disputes, over 50 per cent, both in Great Britain and in the United States, are involved in disputes about wages. Such strikes are but a pale index of the discontent and dissatisfaction among the workers resulting from their belief that their wages are unduly low.

But low wages have an influence on conditions making for war not only in a national aspect, that is, not only in a particular country, but also internationally and in the connection with national differences in standards of living. While the standard of living does not depend wholly on the wage earned, the wage earned is a convenient way of indicating the standard of life. Now the statistics compiled by the International Labour Office showing the index numbers of real wages in various countries indicate surprising differences in these levels of real wages. If the index number of real wages in Great Britain be represented by 100, the figures for certain other countries are as follows: Australia, 148; Austria, 52; Canada, 165; Czechoslovakia, 74; Denmark, 112; Estonia, 45; France, 58; Germany, 77; Irish Free State, 97; Italy, 43; Netherlands, 87; Poland, 65; Spain, 45; Sweden, 113; United States, 197. These figures take into account not merely the money wage earned by the worker but its real purchasing power. We may interpret these figures by saying that the worker in Great Britain is more than twice as well off as the worker in Estonia, Italy or Spain, that he is about one and one-third times as well off as the worker in Germany, but that he is only half as well off as the worker in the United States.

If the standard of living of the workers in the United States, Canada, and Australia is so much above that of the workers in certain European countries, the question may be asked why the workers do not leave their own countries and go to America or Australia. The answer is that they would like to go, but various things make it difficult. In the first place, the immigration regulations of the United States make it possible for only a small proportion of those who would like to enter America to do so. In the second place, language difficulties are important. The worker in Milan or in Warsaw might be better off in Copenhagen or in Stockholm, but he would probably find it an insuperable obstacle to acquire the language of the country to which he went, and a skilled man in a particular trade would not easily get a job unless he knew something of the language of the country to which he went. Finally, family ties exert a strong pressure in favour of the workers remaining where they are. It has often been observed that even within the limits of a particular country, labour tends to be immobile. Family ties and the surroundings that are familiar exert a strong centripetal influence and keep a man tied to his own town. This influence is much stronger when it is a question of going from country to country, and particularly of going overseas. Many workers consider that it is better to work for small wages, where they are certain of regular employment, and where they have their friends and relations, than to launch into the unknown. All these reasons explain, partially at least, why labour does not flow to countries where high wages are to be earned with the same rapidity and ease as capital flows to countries where high dividends are to be obtained. The international transfer of capital is extremely easy. In the case of returns on capital there is tending more and more to be a uniform world

standard. One reason why this uniform world
standard is more difficult of attainment in the
case of labour is because labour is less mobile
than capital.

Is then the ideal of attaining to a uniform
world standard of life an essentially Utopian one?
Can anything be done to make possible such a
world standard? The general economic interdependence of the world has a tendency to depress
the standards of life of the worker in industrially
developed countries. This is why so much anxiety
is felt in European countries at the increasing
competition of the new industries of the East.
These industries, working with labour badly paid
and living on a low standard of life, are able in
many cases to compete with industries manned
by workers enjoying a high standard of life, and
there is at least a tendency for such competition
to drag down the standard of life of the workers
in highly industrialised countries. It used to be
believed that a low standard of life may continue
to exist in one country without affecting the
standard of life in other countries; that belief is
no longer possible. Just as typhus in Russia or
cholera in India constitute a danger to the standard of life of the whole world, so do low conditions of work, whether they exist in China or
Europe or America, menace the workers' standard of life everywhere.

There is, perhaps, increasing tendency to recognise that world standards of life can be raised
only by world-wide collaboration. It is the essential function of the International Labour Organisation to raise the standards of life in countries
which have a low standard until they gradually

approximate to those of countries possessing a
high standard. If such world collaboration does
not become increasingly effective, if national inequalities in standards of living tend to crystal-
lise, and if, as is the case, the workers in various
countries become increasingly aware of these
national inequalities, the dangers of war from
this cause will be real and grave. For if the
workers of a country become convinced that their
standard of living is low, and further, that there
is no possibility of securing an improvement in it
because some other country possesses the raw
materials which they need, or contains the empty
territories on which they would like to settle, or
closes its markets to the goods they would like to
export, it needs no stretch of imagination to recognise that they might readily be induced to
attempt, by war, to obtain what negotiation has
failed to secure.

7. CONCLUSIONS

All the industrial and labour influences making
for war would appear ultimately to be of three
kinds. They are due either to the nature of the
modern industrial order, or to a lack of balance
between production and consumption, or to bad
conditions of work. These influences may contribute to war either by leading to a conflict of
national economic interests, or by giving rise
among the workers to unrest, discontent, demoralisation, and it may be, revolt.

In no instance do these industrial and labour
influences lead directly to war. They do, however,
constitute the raw materials out of which war

may be produced. In all cases alike, in so far as
the peace of the world is threatened, it is because
there is considered to be, explicitly or implicitly,
an infringement of the principles of social justice.
In the first case social justice as between States
or between great interests in different States is
the issue; in the second case conditions exist in-
consistent with the principles of social justice in
the relations of wide classes within the community. Injustice in the relation between States
is not essentially dissimilar from injustice between groups within the same State, or from injustice between individuals. In all cases alike,
justice is essentially social.

The fundamental idea in social justice is the
conception of a synthesis of opposing claims.
Justice does not involve simply the absence of
conflicting points of view. This would be a negative conception. It is something positive, and implies the ultimate conciliation of differences, the
unification of fragmentary aspects of the truth.
Social justice is not ultimately consistent with
conflicts, explicit or latent, involved in bad conditions of labour.

Is it possible to do anything concrete to promote the realisation of social justice? Is it possible to do anything to prevent labour and
industrial influences from leading to war? Is it
possible to do anything to transmute these influences into influences making for peace? Any
attempt to answer these questions, however
briefly, must take into account the special characteristics of each of the particular influences to
which attention has been devoted in this report.

Certain of the influences making for war are due, we have seen, to the nature of the industrial order. Must these influences always result from the nature of the industrial order? Is the industrial order itself changing and is it capable of still further change? The answer would appear to be that changes, in some cases slow, in others rapid, are at all times taking place in the nature of the industrial order, and that those which are at present occurring would appear on the whole to be susceptible of being made to contribute to the ends of peace. One example may be taken. The analysis of the industrial order showed that the centralisation of industry was a characteristic containing within it the seeds of unrest, social revolution, and war. It is therefore particularly important to note that tendencies are already at work within the industrial order itself which will inevitably lead to the gradually increasing decentralisation of industry and to an accompanying decentralisation of population.

The tendencies which are already contributing to the decentralisation of industry are not difficult to discern. The first is the growth of land values in urban areas. The point has already been reached in many urban areas in the United States, Great Britain, France, Germany, and other industrial countries, in which it is more economical for the industrialist to build and work his factory at some distance from a great city. A second important influence making for decentralisation is the rapidly increasing use of electricity as the main source of power. Just as the use of coal led to centralisation, the use of electricity is leading to decentralisation, and electricity is the great source of power of the future. Electricity can be conveyed long distances more cheaply than any other source of power, and in countries where extensive use has been made of it for the provision of power in manufacturing processes the tendency towards a decentralisation of industry has been marked. The third influence in favour of decentralisation is improvement in transport. Cheap and rapid transport permits of the establishment of factories at a distance from the raw materials which they use and also from the markets which they supply. It is important to note that the improvement of transport, in addition to facilitating the decentralisation of industrial production, renders easier the decentralisation of population. As a result of continued improvements both in collective and individual passenger transport, it is now possible for the workers to live at long distances from their work. For example, in one firm in Germany workers live as far as 40 kilometres from the place of work. The decentralisation of population resulting from and accompanying the decentralisation of industrial production makes for improvement in the conditions of life and thus constitutes an important contribution to the ends of peace.

In the case of machine production and factory discipline—the two further characteristics of the industrial order which we found to contain influences making for war—it is worth noting that much is being done by improved technique to avoid the monotony and fatigue to which they give rise.

When we turn to the influences due to lack of balance between production and consumption, we find ourselves in an area in which valuable research is at present being carried on. If the intensive study now being made by economists, statisticians, bankers, and others into the technique of world economic balance through planning were more closely co-ordinated, there can be little doubt that the world would devise measures for securing greater equilibrium between its powers of consumption and its capacity to produce.

Further, bad conditions of work are, simply because they are bad, always susceptible of improvement. Recent years have undoubtedly seen real progress. Hours have been shortened, wages have been raised, and in many countries, by the introduction of systems of social insurance, a measure of security has been added to the satisfaction that the worker now enjoys.

Finally, something is being done in the industrial world, as in other spheres of human experience, to substitute the spirit of co-operation for that of competition. This substitution reposes on psychology rather than on economics. The question is not one of a harsh antithesis between individualist and socialist doctrines. It is rather a matter of psychology. Competition, whether in the industrial or in the political field, is essentially based on the instinct of pugnacity. Now, though the instinct of pugnacity is an ultimate element in the constitution of human nature, it is capable of modification, and the direction of its operation and even its manner of functioning may be changed. The tendency of the instinct of pugnacity to issue, in its elementary form, in socially undesirable manifestations, has suggested to many States the advantage of consciously developing it in the direction of emulation. Emulation is obviously not the same thing as pugnacity, but it is closely related to it. The active encouragement of this impulse is undertaken by the modern State at all levels. In certain countries it forms the basis of the whole educational system. Education is regarded as a formation of character rather than as a storing of the mind with knowledge, and the modern school is therefore, from first to last, organised on an emulative basis.

In international relations, a determined effort is being made to substitute emulation for pugnacity. The events of 1914–1918 showed more clearly than ever before that the hopes that had been entertained that in international relations the instinct of pugnacity would decay through disuse had been based on false assumptions. These years showed, indeed, that the instinct, though latent, had lost none of its force. One of the main aims of the League of Nations is to render pugnacity really unnecessary in international relations. Just as custom has, in civilised States, transmuted by a sort of social alchemy pugnacity into emulation, with the result that physical combat between individuals is rare, so in the international realm the lessons of history suggest that it will be possible, through the development of international law and international administrative machinery, to substitute for physical combat some expression of international emulation.

III

RACIAL INFLUENCES

By C. F. ANDREWS

The word "race" as used in this Report

BEFORE attempting any detailed analysis of the racial influences that make for war, it is necessary to explain what the Commission understands by the word "race". No strict definition is possible, for the evidence appears to be complete that mankind has roamed over the earth for unknown myriads of years and an intermingling has gone on which would make a "pure" race (in the sense of one that has never mingled its blood with any other) unthinkable. It has been decided to aim rather at a practical than a scientific definition, and to use the word "race" in its ordinary sense as applied to those groups of mankind having traits and characteristics which point back to a common history and cultural tradition. At the same time it is clearly understood, that such race distinctions are not ultimate, and that there is in reality only one race of mankind—the human race.

With this general definition before it, the Commission has dealt in its Report with those racial disturbances and anomalies which tend to destroy peace and goodwill among men. Whenever these disturbed racial feelings—artificially stimulated by a sense of political insecurity on the one side and leading to a sense of great injustice on the other—are excited by social and economic inequalities of a galling character, then in the long run violence is likely to break forth and the danger of war to become imminent.

To clarify the subject, the Commission chose as the theme of its deliberations the following question:

"To what extent and in what manner is race a cause of war or a complication leading to war?"

In order to prevent possible misunderstanding, the Commission wishes to preface all that may be related concerning racial friction in this Report with an emphatic positive statement that in the present stage of human development racial differentiation, when not distorted or artificially excited, has a necessary and important part to play which must on no account be lost sight of. Therefore, while dealing with the harm caused to mankind by acute racial animosity, we must constantly remember that there are other aspects of "race" which make for peace and goodwill and are therefore of the highest value. For the marked differences, due to racial manners and customs, which have become inherited and handed down through many generations, have given variety and colour to human life which otherwise might have become dull and drab and monotonously uniform. With regard to such racial distinctions, there is a race pride which is altogether commendable, so long as it does not seek to degrade the pride of other races. There is also a racial character slowly built up which forms a valued inheritance for each individual who belongs to the race. Through such an inheritance the human race, as a whole, makes progress. All these and other advantages of "race" are quite compatible with the absence of racial friction and animosity. Indeed, it is only under conditions of racial harmony and equality that the most treasured varieties of racial experience, which help to build up humanity, can be developed.

The consensus of opinion within the Commission is that the race problem, owing to which world disturbances have occurred, is primarily a political and economic problem rather than a purely biological one, that racial causes of friction which may eventually lead to war are due not to any instinctive and innate antipathies —making differences of race an inevitable cause of repulsion or hostility—but that these outward racial differences have in the past been used as a political weapon by groups of individuals who desired to attain their own selfish ends; that thus there has grown up in certain parts of the world (but not in others) an historic tradition of race antagonisms. This historic sentiment has been used, and mob emotion has been excited, to serve political ends. The fact that, normally, little children do not share these race antagonisms was pointed out as an indication that such antipathies are not innate.

With these preliminary observations, we pass to the main body of the report, which has been arranged under the following headings:

F

Part I. *General considerations* are put forward which are illustrated by typical examples.

Part II. *Different areas* of the world are examined in order to discover the extent of racial friction in those areas.

Part III. *Special Problems* leading to *Racial Friction* are considered.

Part IV. *Conclusions* and *Recommendations* of the Commission.

PART I

SOME GENERAL CONSIDERATIONS CONCERNING RACE

(A) There have been in recent times very important new factors in connection with the problems of "race", which have gravely affected the world situation as a whole. These are likely to lead to inevitable conflict if not forestalled by preventive and remedial measures.

Modern engineering and rapid locomotion, combined with scientific inventions, have for the first time in history overcome very nearly all the difficulties which had previously barred the way to interracial communications. There has come about a shrinkage both of time and space, such as our forefathers would never have conceived to be possible. In all probability, we are on the eve of still greater discoveries, including world television, and world telephonic communication. Yet along with all this there has been an altogether inadequate human adjustment. New forces have been suddenly let loose without control. Races have been brought near to one another without any preparation for mutual readjustment of

standards of living. Misery similar to that which
came a century ago, when the age of coal and
steam broke upon a startled and unprepared
Western world, is likely to come to Africa and the
East in our own day. To take a typical example,
the rubber plantations and mining industries of
Central Africa have already broken up the old
tribal life, without putting anything in its place
which may uphold the moral sanctions. The races
of the East have begun bitterly to feel the economic exploitation of the West.

There has been an altogether unprecedented
growth in human population. The world of man
has doubled its numbers in a single century. Certain countries, such as Great Britain, Ireland,
Germany, Italy, and Japan, have been forced at
different periods either to send their citizens
abroad or else to become highly industrialised at
home. The latter course (as will be seen later)
creates problems of racial adjustment almost as
hard to solve as the former. All the available areas
of land still open for expansion are being very
rapidly filled up. The United States of America
and other countries have been compelled to re-
strict immigration on a quota basis. Manchuria is
still comparatively vacant in the Far East, but its
absorption of new population at a million a year
must soon come to an end. Already this "swarm-
ing" process in human history has begun to reach
its limits, and the racial maladjustment caused by
it is likely rather to increase than to grow less.

Modern industrialism, with its intensive exploitation of raw materials and its concentration
of human labour in crowded areas, has been
carried forward in a manner quite new in the

annals of the human race. It has led inevitably
to over-production for home consumption and,
therefore, to imperial economic expansion abroad.
"Trade follows the flag" has become a watchword. This has brought an entirely new incentive
into the aggressive side of modern national life.
Speeches are constantly made by statesmen
urging the acquisition of colonies for the purposes
of expanding trade and increasing population. If
examples were needed, showing the effect of such
imperialist designs on the subject peoples of the
world, the racial antipathy that has been roused
in opposition to it in Africa and the East is itself
a witness. For it is obvious that, in an already
crowded world, such imperialism can only be
carried into effect by means of the exploitation
and subjection of the weaker races.

(B) Although it may be difficult in modern
times to point to wars that are purely racial in
character—parallel to the tribal wars in the past
—yet it is evident to-day that the racial factor is
entering into and complicating situations which
are already overstrained, and thus tending very
seriously to endanger world peace. Meanwhile a
peculiar bitterness has been added to the struggle.
For example, the national movements in the East
in our own times have become almost fiercely
aggressive owing to the racial bitterness that
often lies behind it. The economic issue on the
Pacific Coast, which might be satisfactorily
settled by a "Gentleman's Agreement", becomes
complicated when it is combined with an Asiatic
Exclusion Act deliberately framed on racial lines.
The religious dispute in Palestine between Jew
and Arab might be amicably settled if there were

not an economic and political struggle in the
background, and an appeal to race feeling always
near at hand.

When we endeavour to make an analysis of
the methods whereby the different races of mankind, overlapping one another in a single area,
have sought to achieve their own solution for the
problems that arise, two opposite methods are
seen to have prevailed in separate areas, and from
these the following evidence may be drawn:

Race segregation was attempted in ancient
India by a cruel system called "untouchability",
whereby the conquered, darker race was tabu as
unclean, and all forms of outward contact with it
were avoided. In modern times a scarcely less
cruel tabu has been placed in certain parts of the
world upon the African Negro race in order to
prevent any social contact taking place on equal
terms.

There are other conditions of segregation also
practised, which are much less harsh than these.
For instance, an area is sometimes reserved for
primitive races, which the Government protects
against encroachment, in order that the primitive
social and tribal life may not be destroyed, and
the land exploited by the European intruder.
Again, the European, on his side, has sometimes
made a reservation of vast unoccupied areas of
the world's surface, and thus, as it were, segre-
gated himself. The occupation and possession of
territory in Australia and Canada, as it has taken
place in modern times, might be mentioned as
an instance. Here, the European race has prevented any non-European either from permanent
residence or even from entering the country by

immigration from across the sea. What has been
called bluntly the "White Australia" policy comes
under this heading.

A modified form of segregation may be observed in India among the higher castes where
intermarriage is strictly forbidden by religion,
but social intercourse is allowed. Here the different castes meet freely and share the same soil,
but only segregate themselves from one another
where marriage relations are concerned. In
ancient Hebrew civilisation the same prohibition
with regard to intermarriage with other races was
widely observed.

The exact opposite of all this has been very
largely practised in many quarters of the world
both in ancient and modern times. In the Roman
Empire, for instance, intermixture of races appears to have been very freely practised. In the
Far East also we find no barriers established
against intermarriage among the races in China.
In the Islamic world, from the very first, intermarriage has been encouraged among those who
have belonged to the same faith. Once more, we
know from historical records that concubinage
was very widely prevalent in the Eastern world, as
well as in the mediaeval West. This has necessarily
implied race fusion. Thus with rare exceptions
intermixture went on all over the world. Indeed,
the refusal of intermarriage was in all probability
never observed so widely as race mixture. In the
modern age, also, while racial segregation with a
view to preventing intermixture of certain races
is practised in North America, Australia, South
Africa, and partially in India, on the other hand,
in South America race fusion by intermarriage is

quite common, and in many other parts of the world there is no social or religious barrier set up against it.

Furthermore, it is possible to point to certain areas where racial contact of the closest kind has occurred without either race mixture or artificial race segregation. For instance, in the British Colonies, where indentured labourers have gone from India in great numbers, it has been the rarest possible event hitherto for a Hindu to marry out of his own caste circle. Intermarriage seems to be inhibited by his social system. It has yet, however, to be seen how long this state of equilibrium will last, and how far new economic, social, or religious causes will tend to break it down. It is noticeable, for example, in this regard, that whenever the Indian immigrants change their religion, the old Hindu inhibition against intermarriage weakens and intermarriage between the races becomes possible. Among those professing Islam, for instance, racial intermingling is both natural and frequent.

It will be necessary at a later stage in this Report to return to this vexed question of intermarriage, because it is probably in this direction that colour and race prejudice, rising at last to a fanatical pitch, has done most mischief. Race repulsion has been created and also propagated sedulously by organised movements which are ready to apply force in the form of active violence to prevent race fusion.

The sanctions which have been mentioned above to prevent intermarriage have often proved, in the long run, not only unfair in themselves, but have also led on to ever-increasing injustice.

They will have to be drastically revised if racial
friction is to be prevented and race harmony is
to prevail. For example, the weapon of social or
religious tabu has sometimes been practised with
exceeding harshness among the Hindus all over
India, and also among the Syrian Christians in
South India. It has led to a burning sense of
injustice where even water from wells has been
prohibited. Again, in South Africa, restriction of
areas wherein trade may be carried on has been
frequently practised or attempted with a view
to racial segregation. Strict separation has been
made in railway and steamer accommodation.
Churches have been set apart for certain races
only. Similar phenomena are found in the
Southern States of America. These sanctions have
become crystallised by use until they have appeared to possess all the force of customary law.

A still further stage has been reached, when
discriminatory legislation has been passed by the
State itself which penalises the weaker races. For
instance, the Colour Bar Act, in South Africa,
prohibits certain races from undertaking skilled
mechanical work which may be notified under
the Act. The greatest of all injustices is per-
petrated when the children of one race are penal-
ised in their education in comparison with those
of the race in power. For this inevitably handi-
caps not only the present generation but the
future also. A vicious circle is entered, from
which there appears to be practically no escape
except by an appeal to some outside power for
assistance.

Whenever this feeling of racial superiority
enters along with its correlative, racial inferior-

ity, every outward difference tends to become
exaggerated on either side. A complex is reached.
For this feeling of superiority is apt to be en-
forced by further actions which are galling to the
weaker race. There follows either an imposition
by force of the language and customs of the
"superior" race upon the weaker; or, on the other
hand, the attempt is made (as already mentioned)
to exclude the weaker race in such a way as to
insult and humiliate it. Then, so long as the
weaker race is able to resist, it will carry on the
conflict. But it may be forced to give way, and
thus become one of the downtrodden and suppressed races. Since such suppression of a weaker
race by a stronger has often resulted in the
multiplication of the progeny of the weaker race,
the effort to suppress by force the rapidly multi-
plying weaker race has become intensified. This
has led to ever-increasing cruelty being per-
petrated. The ultimate problem of world peace
has always been how to break through these
vicious circles and restore human justice, without recourse to violence. Contempt on the side
of the stronger race must ultimately meet with
a growing resentment from the side of the weaker
race, which becomes immediately manifest whenever the weaker race has not been reduced to
impotence by the application of brute force. The
only feasible way to deal with such a situation,
and thus either forestall an outbreak of violence
or else remove a long-standing and cruel suppression, is to endeavour to obtain the consent
of the stronger side in the dispute to submit the
questions of injustice to a World Court of Arbitration. Even to suggest such a solution, in the

present state of world public opinion, may appear to be a counsel of perfection. But an analogy has now been created by the procedure of the League of Nations, whereby minorities may claim from the League protection and justice. Though the beginning already made in this direction under the League may seem to be insignificant, it points to a development of human thought which may still have a great future before it. The International Court of Justice at the Hague, and the League of Nations at Geneva, have clearly only commenced to function in human affairs, and it can be proved to be entirely illogical to take action about the wrongs suffered by "minority" fragments of nations, and to pay no attention to the cruelties practised upon "suppressed" races. It can be shown that this aspect of world peace was not overlooked when the Covenant of the League was established by reference to Article XXIII (b) in which the members of the League undertake to secure just treatment of the native inhabitants of territories under their control.

(C) Where one culture, which may be racial in character, has gone rapidly in advance with its own skill and learning and civilisation, then sometimes it clashes with a primitive culture; and weapons of war are ready at hand with which to destroy it. The race that is more advanced in the arts of civilisation will put forward the plea of necessity. Segregation may in the end be attempted from the side of the higher culture, where the primitive race cannot be suppressed by force, or where its customs cannot be violently changed. Examples of these processes may be found in Africa at the present time.

(D) Lastly, religion itself has produced, and may again produce, this vicious circle leading directly to war. Even highly ethical religions may weaken their own case by an appeal to force under the plea of necessity or of self-preservation. This may be seen in the early tendency of many progressive religions. The fear of contamination by vicious moral customs among those differing in religious belief has often in the past become an exciting cause of war. Even though religious wars have not been practised in this manner during recent historic times, nevertheless, the hostile sentiment still remains wherever the superiority of one religion over another is emphasised in a sensational manner by modern methods of propaganda, and where a more primitive moral code is condemned by the intellectual standards of a higher culture.

A common feature of racial frictions of this kind is that the race which claims its own superiority is accustomed to use degrading and insulting epithets about the weaker race, in order thus to excuse an aesthetic and even a moral repugnance. Examples of this may be found in the use of the word "white", as contrasted with the word "black", which often implies an entirely unjustified moral connotation. This racial dislike may be of the most trivial character; it may even be purely imaginary. But irrational prejudice, thus artificially stimulated, is frequently wont to act as a tabu, and sometimes even reaches the pitch of physical repulsion. It would appear that in these extreme instances there is not seldom a morbid psychological background, and possibly even a birth inheritance which is quite irrational, but at the same time cannot be overcome without extreme difficulty. This may point back to some long and bitter conflict in the past, when the two races fought each other ruthlessly. For instance, the repulsion which is so strong in South Africa may possibly have originated in the hard struggles and bloodthirsty raids of bygone days. When the mental inhibition has gone as deep as that, it is necessary to wean the mind from its inherited weakness gradually by education, and by an appeal to the religious motive. Such an appeal has quite recently been made with effect, at a time of religious revival in South Africa. For in the recent visit of the group called the Oxford Fellowship, remarkable testimony was given as to release from this racial inhibition, and the creation in the mind of an entirely new outlook on the racial question. Such an instance has its remarkable bearing on the subject of this International Conference which aims at world peace through religion.

PART II

RACE FRICTION IN DIFFERENT AREAS OF THE WORLD

CHINA

Strong racial antipathies of an instinctive character do not appear to be at all common among the Chinese people. They are not easily excited by passions of this kind and generally keep good humour and courtesy when dealing with foreign people. There is very little dislike of intermarriage with other races. A democratic ideal is widely prevalent among the village people, which makes for social and racial equality.

Yet at the same time there is a profound and deep-seated traditional sense of cultural superiority. This has revealed itself in Chinese history from a far distant past, and it still prevails to-day. China was regarded by the Chinese as the "Middle Kingdom". It was looked upon as the centre of world civilisation. Wherever, therefore, the fear has arisen that the foreigner was bent on overthrowing the indigenous culture of China, an active antipathy has been created against the foreigner, which has become racial in character. The methods of forceful economic penetration employed by the West against China have aroused among the Chinese themselves such opposition that they have resulted in widespread popular uprisings, combined with a violent hatred of the foreigner. This antipathy culminated in the Boxer Rising leading to untold misery. If, however, the Chinese were allowed to develop their own country in their own manner, even though there might be internal dissensions, there would be no serious likelihood of China disturbing the peace of other nations or becoming imperial in her aims. What is most needed at the present time in this connection, in order to avoid the danger of serious disturbance in the Far East, is the relief of the economic pressure of the West upon China, and a recognition of China's right to manage her own internal affairs.

Furthermore, a fundamental change in world perspective is urgently needed. The greatness of Chinese art, literature, civilisation, and history,

for instance, has to be fully recognised and acknowledged. A similar revision of popular ideas
concerning Western civilisation is also needed on
the part of China. The old "barbarian" idea concerning the West has to be abandoned. On both
sides, this mutual disdain should disappear, and
a true historical and cultural appreciation should
be encouraged by careful study.

This should begin in the primary schools on
both sides of the world, and a thorough revision
of historical and geographical text-books should
be undertaken. A further point of exceptional
importance would be the exchange of teachers,
students, and research workers. An intelligent and
well-organised promotion of residential study, research, and lecture work abroad would be of the
greatest value as a contribution towards world
peace. It would not, however, be sufficient merely
to invite students and teachers from China to
the West and *vice versa*. There is needed at the
same time a carefully organised effort to make
residence in the West by Chinese students and
teachers accompanied by those amenities and
friendly relations which would make it possible
for the Eastern visitors to appreciate fully the
best of the Western civilisation, so that they may
be able rightly to interpret its meaning when they
return to their own shores. One such living in-
terpreter can do much to remove wrong ideas
and create goodwill even where bitterness existed
before.

JAPAN

It would appear from the evidence given that
the racial feeling in Japan towards the neigh-

bouring people on the continent of Asia has never
become strong enough to generate a permanent
racial antipathy. Wars on either side have been
those of imperial conquest and invasion, such as
find their parallel in the history of Europe. At
the same time, in Korea and China, in recent
years there has been a constant fear of Japan's
superior force, which has led to great bitterness.
Japan, on the other hand, has always readily
acknowledged her cultural debt to China, and also
to India. The ancient Chinese classics still form
one of the main backgrounds of Japanese art and
culture. In this respect Japan has felt the reverent
regard of a younger civilisation towards its own
older cultural teachers. Any trouble that may
have arisen in this direction has been political
rather than racial. Even the economic boycott of
Japan by China, which has been severely felt, has
been taken, on the whole, calmly, and has not disturbed racial feelings.[1]

On the other side of the Pacific, however, the
antipathy to Japan in America, which expressed
itself bluntly and crudely in the Asiatic Exclusion Act of 1924, and also by continual instances of racial discrimination along the Pacific
Coast of North America, has been resented with
an intensity of feeling difficult to understand in
the United States. It was impossible for a country
so proud of its own traditions as Japan to receive
such humiliating treatment from America without a strong and painful reaction. Japan has,

[1] Though this was written before the recent outbreak of
hostilities at Shanghai, it may still be argued the causes of
the Sino-Japanese conflict are political and economic and are
not inspired by racial animosity.—EDITOR.

however, shown little inclination to think of retaliation. Nevertheless, what has been hard to bear patiently has been the imputation of racial inferiority, which the present attitude of the West towards Japan implies. This was brought to a direct issue at the Peace Conference in 1919, when Japan endeavoured to obtain the principle of racial equality embodied in the Covenant of the League of Nations, but found this opposed by Western Powers. In keeping with this refusal, the "White Australia" policy, though economic in its origin, has also appeared to Japan to have a racial basis.

An immigration into Brazil, where no race or colour prejudice is prevalent, is now being attempted from Japan—with the enthusiasm of the whole nation behind it. But it is still too early to judge whether it is likely to prove successful.

INDIA

The most complex and difficult racial problems have been presented by India. From time immemorial the races of the East have gravitated towards this fertile land, which lies behind the Himalayas in the full track of the monsoon. In very early days, an energetic people called Dravidians, having their own culture, language, and art, passed over the whole of the south of India and settled there in great numbers, supplanting the aboriginals, and forming kingdoms of their own. At a later date, the Aryans invaded the country from the north and penetrated southward. After them, at different times, various warlike tribes poured in from Central Asia, spreading

towards the west by way of Rajputana and
Gujerat. Later still, the Moslem invaders belong-
ing to many races settled in India, especially in
the north. Those Hindus who joined the fold of
Islam and adopted its institutions and manners
intermarried with them. Last of all, the Europeans
entered India by way of the sea.

Thus races of entirely different origin have
invaded India time after time and settled on
Indian soil. The problem of racial adjustment
has been one of the chief determining factors in
the making of Indian history. Its solution has
been mainly attempted among the Hindus by
a peculiar method called the caste system. As
already mentioned, religious sanctions were introduced in Hindu India to prevent intermarriage,
while the races remained side by side without
wars of extermination such as had taken place in
other countries. Thus the invading tribes in early
Indian history became automatically absorbed
in the social organisation as separate castes and
sub-castes, each forming a fresh unit. These
units kept their own marriages religiously confined within their own caste boundaries, maintaining at the same time social intercourse in
other directions. Inter-dining, however, was prohibited as a further safeguard against intermarriage. The peculiar genius of the Hindu religion worked itself out along these lines.

What can be said for this Hindu attempt to
solve the race problem is that it allowed a definite
place for each race and did not involve continual
internecine wars. It offered its own solution also
to the intermarriage problem. But it has undoubtedly resulted in very great evils, which

G

Indian thinkers and statesmen have been the
first to recognise. All through mediaeval and
modern India there have been movements of
religious revolt and reformation. Within Hinduism itself, from every side, religious leaders have
arisen whose teaching has tended to modify the
rigid lines of the caste system. Raja Ram Mohan
Roy was the earliest and best-known among those
whose reforms frankly contemplated a harmony
of East and West. He was followed by others
whose influence permeated Bengal and indirectly
extended over other parts of India. Swami Daya-
nanda Saraswati, the founder of the Arya Samaj,
still further loosened the rigid bonds of the caste
system in the north of India. By making caste
functional, rather than a birth inheritance, he
made it possible to bring the outcastes, after
purification, within the caste system. The Ramakrishna Mission strictly followed the teaching of
Swami Vivekananda, who preached as his gospel
that God was to be found especially among the
poor (Daridra-Narayan). This religious movement
has sent its monks to work among the sufferers,
however low they may have been depressed in
their social standing. Mahatma Gandhi, in his
turn, taking up the same doctrine as a practical
religious and social reformer, has by his own
personal example done more than anyone else in
modern times to counteract the evil of "untouchability" which had become unduly associated with the caste system of Hinduism. The poet
Rabindranath Tagore has been fearless in his own
active repudiation of the evils of caste, and has in
his own person broken through caste regulations.
His writings have done most of all in modern

Indian literature to bring these evils before the bar of public conscience.

While much may be said with truth concerning the progress that has thus been made, nevertheless the segregation of the "untouchables"—preventing them even from drawing water from wells or entering temples or meeting with their fellow-men on equal terms—still prevails in the south and west of India, and also in Orissa, and to a lesser extent elsewhere. It thus may be said to represent one of the greatest injustices still unremedied in India.

With regard to the Europeans, who came across the sea into India, there appears to have been, in the first instance, no racial antipathy felt either on account of their colour or their religion and culture. But in recent times, owing to disturbed political conditions and the humiliation involved in subjection, Indians are beginning to be aware of a racial consciousness among themselves which cuts across the barriers of their own castes and creeds, putting national units first. This is reaching the villages as well as the towns. It is tending to weld the diverse classes of India's population into a united whole. In so far as this becomes effective, the evils of "untouchability" are likely still further to decrease and the rigidity of the caste system will be relaxed.

South Africa

South Africa, to-day, is singularly akin to India with regard to its own acute racial problems. In certain marked respects it is attempting the very same methods of solution. Segregation is being tried on a large scale, which includes nearly the whole of life; and the dangers of miscegenation are being preached with a religious fervour. But, in this modern instance, there has been added to the racial segregation an ingrained "colour" prejudice, that has gradually become one of the dominating features of the whole situation. While it may be true that colour distinction marked off originally the caste people in India from the outcaste—as the Sanskrit term *varna* seems to denote—this original aspect of caste, as a distinct colour prejudice, died out in India with the extinction of colour groups. There is no actual colour complex in India to-day such as we find in South Africa and in the south of the United States.

The gravest racial crisis in the present generation is met with in South Africa. There the Bantus have been deprived of their land to such an extent that they have become literally "hewers of wood and drawers of water" for the Europeans. The line of colour is starkly drawn and an attempt is being made to perpetuate it by means of legal enactments. Yet at the same time efforts are being made to ameliorate these conditions, as referred to elsewhere in this Report.

Central Africa

Central Africa is still in many respects, as a focus of racial evils, one of the darkest spots on the map of the world. The wrongs of the old slave raiding have not been altogether obliterated even though open slavery has ceased. This oppressively tropical area of the globe, infested with

deadly diseases, seems to depress all those who
dwell in it. There is a savagery in Nature which
has its reflex in man. Among the living races of
mankind, the aboriginals of Tropical Africa,
especially in the Congo basin, have been dragged
down by unhealthy climatic conditions, and also
by degrading superstitions; and they have in turn
dragged down those who have exploited them for
labour purposes.

Amid much that is sinister in these regions,
there is one factor that gives ground for hope.
If the diseases of the tropics, which enfeeble and
undermine the human frame, can be overcome
and healthy conditions can be maintained for
several generations, then a basis of physical fitness may at last be established, which might be
built upon by improved education and by the
vital spirit of religion. In this way, the wounds
inflicted by centuries of slavery and massacre
may be healed, and the present racial contempt,
mingled with crude colour prejudice which so
often overtakes the members of the European
race who trade there, might be modified and
changed. For if education could be advanced on
intelligent lines, and at the same time the latent
religious impulses of the African find expression,
then it might be hoped that the musical and
artistic gifts of the Negro would attain their full
scope in creative ways in Africa, as they have
done in the United States of America. In that
case, a growing respect for the African would
take the place of contempt, and the whole basis
of colour prejudice, which originally started in
Africa, would be undermined. Mutual esteem
would grow stronger instead of mutual dislike.

It might be hoped that in time the question of colour among human beings would not arise, to ruin the possibility of mutual kindly relations. Convincing evidence was presented to the Commission of the vital strength of the religious impulse among the Central African tribes and of its power to transform human life.

THE UNITED STATES OF AMERICA

While it is still true to-day that the race and colour prejudice, which has led to the segregation of the Bantu in South Africa, has its counterpart in the southern portion of the United States in the treatment of the American Negro, and while the savage barbarity of lynching has not yet been finally stopped, yet at the same time in that country since the abolition of slavery an advance has been made in the uplift and education of the whole Negro race which is likely to improve automatically his status to a degree that would have hardly seemed possible a generation ago. A paper was given to the Commission containing the statement made to General Smuts by the American Negro leaders at Washington early in 1930. It showed with convincing clearness how religious influences had proved, in the early stages, the main factor in creating and supporting the progressive *will* within the Negro Community. This will for improvement had manifested itself in a profound eagerness for education and enlightenment. It gave the moral character and determination necessary to overcome all obstacles in order to obtain the best education that could be had. The life of Mr.

Booker Washington served to illustrate this point. On the other hand, reactionary religious forces in the Southern States, giving sanction to race prejudice, have proved one of the main obstacles standing in the way of Negro progress.

From this paper it would be possible to draw the conclusion that when a race is backward or oppressed, it can still obtain the power to overcome initial opposition and eliminate one injustice after another by the sheer force of its own inner character. This happens when that character itself is strengthened and moulded by deep religious convictions. Thus, for the purpose of the World Conference for Peace through Religion, the findings of this gathering of Negro leaders at Washington are of great importance. They show, in a remarkably clear way, what the religious motive is able to effect in order to achieve by peaceful and non-violent means better racial relations, especially at the outset of the struggle, when conditions of advance are hardest of all.

The following summary of a portion of General Smuts' speech at the end of the meeting may be quoted here as follows:

"General Smuts expressed his deep appreciation for a new view on the American race question, his admiration for the sanity, balance and public concern of the Negro leaders and their co-workers in race adjustment. He was particularly impressed with the demonstrated effectiveness of the technique of round-table conferences —a technique common to the new international machinery of the League of Nations and the interracial councils of the United States. Here was one practical way out, as they were beginning to discover in South Africa through their joint Councils."

The statement contained in this paper ends as follows:

"It is not too much to regard this visit from South Africa to the United States as in part a practical expression of a new vision and a new interest, and the reactions of this visit as a constructive contribution, however potential, to a distant racial situation which at present is at an acutely critical stage.

"Certainly the most enlightened thought on the race question has everything to gain by broadening out to an international scope and an international basis of understanding. And that must ultimately work both ways—from America to Africa and from Africa to America as well."

In relation to this statement two points come clearly into prominence which appear to be of very great importance for the World Conference for Peace through Religion. (1) We can trace the vital part that religion itself performs in supplying the motive power to overcome the greatest obstacles in the way of human progress. If world brotherhood is to be established in place of the present racial inequality and injustice, then it is clear from the history of human progress in past ages that all the higher motive forces of religion will be needed to bring about the consummation of our hopes. On this side, the World Conference for Peace through Religion has its own important part to play. (2) The way of Conference and Council has to be substituted for that of war. The "moral equivalent for war" which William James desiderated may possibly be reached in

one direction through the difficult work of adjustment and mutual consideration on a basis of
equality at the council table and in international
conference proceedings. It is here that difficulties
must be solved and obstacles overcome. It will be
evident, therefore, that in this second issue as well
as with regard to the importance of religion itself
as a basis, the World Conference for Peace through
Religion has a vital function to perform.

OTHER RACIAL AREAS

It is not possible within the brief space of this
report to deal in detail with the racial issues in
the Near East and in Eastern Europe, though
their importance for a full study of the subject
is acknowledged. Nor can the South American
situation be taken up in full. The present position in Central Asia under the U.S.S.R. may,
however, be mentioned. It appears not unlikely
that within the Soviet Republics many of the
racial barriers will be surmounted by the uniform
economic system. Colour distinctions are not
observed at all, and in that respect a great
burden is lifted from mankind. A Negro will have
no different treatment in Moscow from that
given to a member of the Caucasian race.

While it is a fact that colour prejudice, as
such, is and has always been singularly absent
from the mental outlook of the Slav in Eastern
Europe, and also from that of the Latin races all
over the world, yet it is by no means a fact
that the economic exploitation of the coloured
races, reducing them to conditions bordering on
serfdom, had been absent where the Latin races

have obtained political control. In Latin America
a state of peonage still exists in nearly every
tropical area, and from this the aboriginals suffer
most of all. In Africa along the Congo, and in
Equatorial regions, the harshest conditions of
racial treatment have prevailed for generations
which show the inherent cruelty of racial
domination over one race by another. The
same cruelty has been witnessed in Angola
and Mozambique under the Portuguese. Indeed,
every conquering race in Africa, whether the
Arab on the eastern coast or the warlike
African tribes themselves—all alike have practised ruthlessness when power has come into
their hands.

A question often raised is whether there exists
any racial prejudice of a marked character between the Indians and the Africans, or between
the Indians and Chinese. Opinion on this point
appears to be divided, and probably the facts
have not yet been sufficiently examined. Some
members of this Commission, who have had an
opportunity to observe the relations of these
races in almost every part of the world, consider
that there is no inherent racial repulsion between
them, and that even in certain circumstances
where there is economic rivalry, there does not
seem to be any marked development of a race
complex. In British Guiana the Indians and
Africans live side by side, without intermarrying,
in a very friendly manner. In South Africa there
is no actual friction between them. With the
Chinese, the Indian immigrants mix freely in
Malaya and elsewhere. There is very little intermarriage and hardly any sign of race friction.

But, on the other hand, the recent clash in Rangoon between the Burmese and Telugu immigrants, which was the climax of a labour rivalry leading unfortunately to bloodshed, has seemed to show racial feeling brought into the dispute. The Burmese labouring classes felt bitterly that they were being ousted by the Telugus from India, and as the bitterness increased it tended to take the form of racial hate.

Throughout the Malay Peninsula and Indonesia, the Chinese race deserves special mention for its uniformly friendly character in racial relations. The Chinese in this part of the world have an instinct for quietly managing their own affairs, and getting on peaceably with other people.

PART III

SPECIAL PROBLEMS LEADING TO RACIAL FRICTION

INTERMARRIAGE AND RACE MIXTURE

Perhaps no single feature of the race problem is more hotly debated and leads to more bitterness in discussion than that of intermarriage between races distinct from one another in feature and far apart in origin and habitation. Some of the historical facts connected with this question have already been dealt with, but it will be well to consider further the problems connected with it, because racial passion and prejudice have frequently resulted from it.

Generally, it may be stated that those who are near in race to one another prefer to intermarry

among themselves, while those who are distant
from one another by race prefer to remain apart
in their marriage relations. Nevertheless, an overlapping of races has constantly taken place,
owing either to conquest or migration; and it is
a truism that the rapidity of modern inter-com-
munication is bringing the world closer together
in our own age. We have further to consider the
future, with its accelerated air transport, decreasing still more the distance between those
races that are widely divergent one from another.
Mankind must inevitably become more and more
intertwined as the centuries pass, and it is im-
probable that the races will remain as far apart
in their marriage relations as they are to-day.

When we turn to the map of the world in
order to see what is actually taking place before
our eyes, we find certain migrating races continually raising up new populations and producing new varieties in the human race. Such a
migrating race is the Chinese, which is now
spreading over South-Eastern Asia and also
northward into Manchuria. But more than any
other, the peoples of crowded Europe have become ubiquitous. In some parts of the world,
such as South America, they have freely mingled
their blood with that of other races; in other parts
they have been in theory rigidly exclusive.

When we come to examine further the question of intermarriage in relation to different races,
we find that repugnance to it hardly exists among
the Latin races. Witness the French, who, along
with the Arab, Berber, and Negro, are forming a
mixed population along the North Coast of Africa
without any demarcating lines of segregation.

The French Empire there, like the Roman Empire before it, will in time contain a mixed population. Its civilisation will be French, but the people in it will be varied and will intermarry freely. This whole attitude towards the problem of race differs materially from that of the Boer and Briton towards the Bantu in South Africa, where the most rigid segregation prevails.

We find something of the same contrast in India, where the caste system imposes a rigid social barrier against intermarriage. This Hindu attitude towards intermarriage may be contrasted with that of the Indian Mussulman, who exercises his own absolute freedom to marry whom he will among all the believers in Islam.

One interesting experiment in racial segregation as a means of preventing intermarriage may be mentioned, which goes by the name of the "White Australia Policy". Along with economic considerations, the racial factor has been uppermost in the minds of those who devised this plan of action. The doctrine of a "White" continent is now held with all the fervour of religion. Yet it is not difficult to realise its essential unfairness to the other neighbouring races, when it forcibly keeps fertile territory empty, in the tropical North Australian belt, without any prospect of permanent "White" residence up to the limit of population that its well-watered soil can easily bear. All the while, important races with cultures of their own, accustomed to the tropical heat, seek to overflow their bounds in India and China, but they are forbidden to occupy these vacant tropical lands though they are not far from their own shores. It should be added that those who maintain most strongly this "White Australia" policy have no compunction at all about residing themselves in the very countries that are prohibited from sending residents to Australia.

So far only the factor of marriage has been touched upon in relation to race mixture, but another element full of sinister consequences incessantly appears where society is built up from its foundation on some immoral economic structure, such as slavery, or serfdom, or the complete domination of one race by another. For the inferiority treatment, accompanied by economic bondage, is bound to lead continually to an illicit gratification of human passion on the part of the stronger race, to which the weaker race easily succumbs. This becomes demoralising both to the parents and their offspring. Nothing is likely to do more to bring intermingling of races into bad repute than the sad results of such illicit unions. If, therefore, the segregation of races were to take place at all, it should only be by mutual consent and for the preservation on either side of their own inheritance. It should never be forced by one race on another.

The brief analysis which has here been given of some of the aspects of this difficult and complicated question of race mingling reveals clearly that sincere opinions, differing very widely indeed from one another, are held in various parts of the world, some favouring entire race integrity and others deliberately contemplating racial mixture. In such circumstances, one thing is becoming more and more apparent. The full historical and scientific knowledge which might throw light upon the racial problem at this point, where amateur opinion is so divided, has never yet been fully collected and explored. Yet all the while an explosive force is being generated within human society which flashes out in lawless acts, such as lynching, and gives rise to such organisations as the Ku-Klux-Klan. This makes it appear imperative that humanity should no longer be left in ignorance where true information is near at hand. For it should not be difficult for scientific knowledge to be gathered and distinguished from pseudo-science, nor for some guidance to be given as to the future.

IMMIGRATION

Closely related to intermarriage is the question of immigration. While at an earlier period of human history it was easy for races to roam freely over the earth, in modern times population, over large tracts, has become so congested that expansion becomes a necessity; yet this expansion may injure the prosperity of other races into whose area migration takes place. On the other hand, empty areas may be selfishly held by force to prevent these rapidly expanding races from entering there for settlement. Meanwhile—as the filling up of the United States of America shows quite clearly—the over-population of the earth's surface has already begun, and the congestion in certain areas where large supplies of minerals or exceedingly fertile soils exist, is likely to become more and more acute. In what is happening to-day there is waste, disorder, and confusion. Matters of very great moment, affecting the future of the human race, are being settled in a haphazard manner by the blind excitement of passion and greed rather than by reasonable actions based on mutual consideration and goodwill. Waste and disorder lead to injustice, and injustice leads to wars.

INTERNATIONAL DISCOURTESY

The questions discussed above point forward directly to a further racial problem which is becoming daily more difficult to solve as the population of the world draws closer together and the races tend to overlap at many points. Courtesy in racial matters is now of far greater urgency than before, because there has never hitherto been such intimate closeness of racial contact. Yet very little notice has been taken of this side of the subject. Since the future of the human race is likely still further to witness congestion of population, the careful teaching of each generation in turn as to the vital necessity of goodwill in dealing with the idiosyncrasies of other people becomes of primary importance. For men have to learn to live together without quarrelling, and this can only be attained by training and practice. Text-books used in schools which give a contemptuous or one-sided description of other races need to be carefully revised.

Not alone, however, through school education must this necessary race-training be given. Those much wider audiences reached by cinema and radio should be rightly instructed about the things that draw races together. How incredibly shortsighted the present generation is, may easily be seen by the moving pictures which are being sent from America and Europe all over the world giving only the coarser side of Western civilisation. The harm already effected by sensational films is incalculable.

In the same manner great evil is done in the matter of common speech by the use of degrading terms, whether in the West or in the East when speaking of different races. Such words casually repeated give serious offence. International courtesy demands great care about little things as well as general goodwill.

FOREIGN RESIDENCE

The full test of courtesy comes when visitors go abroad and have to conduct themselves under watchful observation. The test equally applies to those who belong to a country to which foreign visitors go; for racial goodwill must obviously be mutual.

Mention has been made before the Commission of racial bitterness at Shanghai and other Chinese ports, where Europeans hitherto have tended to keep themselves aloof from the people of the country, except when using them as clerks in their offices and as domestic servants. There have been parks, for instance, at Shanghai where the Chinese themselves were not admitted except as servants of their European masters. This has been felt by the Chinese to be galling in the extreme, because China is their own country. Such conduct as this, which might be found also among Europeans in India and elsewhere, has led, perhaps more than anything else, to that bitter resentment which is the fuel of a racial conflagration.

Evidence has also been given to the Commission

H

that in Great Britain race relations have become less cordial since the number of foreign students from the East has increased. An exclusive attitude is now often found in unexpected quarters. Frequently visitors from the East are refused accommodation in boarding-houses by landladies who are supposedly seeking for paying guests. In Edinburgh it appears to be difficult for students from the East to take part in the social, and even sometimes the athletic, life of the university. They have also to overcome many obstacles as medical students in order to gain admission into the hospitals for medical purposes. This situation does not exist elsewhere in Europe, where Indian students generally receive a friendly welcome.

In the evidence given, a tribute has been paid to the International House at Riverside Drive in New York and kindred institutions in America and England and other countries. At the same time students from the East assert that they frequently find the colour prejudice towards the Negro in the United States directed also against themselves.

On the other hand, it has been pointed out that if the numbers who come from the East—often immature youths—go on increasing every year, without carefully planned organisation to select those who shall come and also to meet them on arrival, then great hardship is certain to be experienced, however desirous a country may be of dealing fairly with the influx. It is bad for the East and West alike, if very young persons come over to Europe or America without friends and are immediately exposed to all the temptations of city life in a strange country far away from home.

Efforts ought to be made from the side of the East to limit the influx each year to students of mature age, who may come to the West for research work and advanced study. There is also needed more organised voluntary effort in order to offer them hospitality on landing and friendly help during those early days in a strange country which are the most difficult of all. Friendship thus offered has often proved to be one of the best solvents of racial friction. Such agencies exist, both in England and America, but their good work needs supplementing.

The Rising Nationalism in the East

The temper of Nationalism is rapidly rising in every country of the East and in certain parts of Africa as well. Therefore, the atmosphere to-day is full of discontent. Inconsiderate racial treatment by Western people, which once was taken passively, is now deeply resented. The old superiority exercised by the Western Powers is no longer acknowledged on the same scale. The prestige of the West has broken down—partly as a result of the War—and its influence over the masses of illiterate villagers in India and elsewhere has passed away, never to be recalled. If these facts are clearly recognised by those who go out to the East, the national movements may go forward without any large increase of racial friction.

But if, on the other hand, this loss of prestige, which has undoubtedly occurred, is resented by Western rulers, and if its recovery be attempted by acts of violent repression, then a racial conflict may arise, ending in war. It is not within the scope of the World Conference for Peace through Religion to enter into these direct political issues, but it is a bounden duty at such critical times to plead earnestly that the Christian religion itself, along with other religions also, has laid down the precept of daily conduct whereby men should do to others what they would wish to be done to themselves. This reciprocal treatment would surely imply that national freedom in the East ought to be not less dear to Western nations than their own freedom. Along the line of this great principle of reciprocity—which is well understood in the East—there is hope that the new uprising of racial animosity may subside; but without this recognition it is likely still further to increase.

The Crushing Wealth of the West

The preponderating material wealth of the West, as contrasted with the extreme poverty of the East, leads to further difficulties which serve to increase race friction. It is almost impossible for those who arrive from the East (except in rare instances) to live for long on a Western scale of expenditure without impoverishing themselves and their families. In spite of admirable efforts made by International Student Service Associations to provide cheap food, etc., the cost of living in Great Britain and America remains almost prohibitive. Even in Germany the difficulties are great, and there a new language has to be learnt. The result has been that misery and destitution often ensue, combined with disappointment and other unfortunate reactions.

The balance of wealth in the world is now heavily loaded against the East, which has neither the machine-power, nor the realised mineral wealth of the West. This leads to a false sense of superiority on the part of the West, and an altogether unnecessary humiliation, in outward circumstances, on the part of the East. This material inequality is felt all the more bitterly because it is combined often with political subjection. The injustice of all this and a rankling sense of wrong is one of the most potent causes of strife.

Economic Imperialism

Furthermore, political control has led to an economic imperialism of an oppressive character, whereby the stronger power by its material resources and scientific equipment is able to exploit for its own use the weakness of the East. It has also been able to force its own industrial civilisation and to some extent its own extravagant standards of living on people entirely unsuited to them. Thus the races of Africa and the Orient have been led by their experience to believe that Europe and America have grown rich at their expense. This has become an almost universal belief and a sense of injustice has been left festering in the mind in consequence. It is not hard to see how such a picture of unequal treatment, kept constantly before people's minds, leads directly to racial friction, whereby East and West are put in direct opposition.

In the Preamble of Part XIII of the Treaty of Versailles the following is written:

"Whereas conditions of labour involving such

injustice, hardship, and privation to large numbers of people as to produce unrest so great that the peace and harmony of the world are imperilled. . . ."

The same Preamble goes on to state that universal peace can only be established if it is based on social justice. The clear implication is that all influences producing social injustice imperil the cause of world peace. This surely applies to racial injustice in an equal manner.

On the other side, it has to be freely acknowledged that the influx of people from the East as labourers into the West in large numbers tends at cnce to lower the wage standard and thus to bring down the standard of living itself in the West. Justice, therefore, demands that care should be paid to this argument in so far as it is well founded. But it is of the utmost importance that questions of racial inferiority should not be mixed up with it. "Gentlemen's Agreements" have served to prevent a racial clash in this direction, and the submission of difficulties to arbitration should still further relieve matters in the future. It should also be pointed out that it is entirely unfair to recruit indentured labour in the East and to import it, as was done in the past by forcible means from Africa, and then afterwards to keep it, when released from servitude or indenture, in a degraded position. When the fault has been committed of importing indentured or slave labour, it can only be rectified by raising, through education, the children of the labourers till they reach the standards of living of the new country where they will remain.

RELIGIOUS IMPERIALISM

In certain areas of the world, missionary religious movements have become involved in, and almost identified with, a religious imperialism, which causes racial friction. Since the number of those who go out as missionaries is very large, it seems to the Commission necessary, while acknowledging the admirable work that is often done, to impress upon the missionary societies the importance, at such a critical time, of exercising the greatest care in the selection and training of candidates. Clearly nothing could less express the spirit and character of Christ than any exhibition of racial arrogance among those who go out to preach in His name. In spite of the presence in the mission field of exceptional characters, leading lives of great simplicity and humility, and thus truly representing their Master, there are still to be found among missionaries those who have greatly embittered Eastern minds by ignorant attacks and foolish controversy, and also by an assumed superiority that provokes all who have come in contact with it. The cause of World Peace through Religion becomes endangered when the representatives of religion themselves provoke ill-will and strife.

It would appear to be of equal importance for authoritative persons in the East to discourage from the outset those who go over to America, professing to be religious *swamis* and *yogis*, in cases where their daily lives clearly belie their assumed profession. Much harm has been done by such fraudulent persons, who are in reality neither saintly nor even honest. A racial dislike

of the East has sometimes followed when gross
hypocrisy, combined with deceit in money
matters, has been discovered behind the thin
veneer of a spiritual profession. These people
make it very hard for genuine religious leaders
from the East—such as those who have come
out in the Ramakrishna Mission—to carry on
their work. Yet it cannot be doubted that the
West needs to become acquainted at first hand
with the religion and culture of the East.

The Fear Complex

The Commission is definitely of the opinion that
the element of fear is one of the chief causes, in the
West and East alike, of racial unrest. Wherever
the labourer's daily livelihood is threatened, there
at once race passion is likely to accentuate the
economic danger. In the seaports of Great Britain
such race conflicts have occurred between British
seamen and foreigners who were taking away their
livelihood by accepting lower wages. Such fear
may be witnessed also on the part of the "poor
whites" in the United States when they see the
rapid advance of the Negro in industrial pursuits.

In relation to this fear as a primary disturbing
cause, Professor Bonn of the Economic Section
of the Commission presents this important historical judgment:

"A great part of the world history can only be
explained by the desire of the saturated States to
maintain their privileged position in regard to
power and wealth, and of non-saturated States
to gain wealth in order to be more powerful, or
to get power in order to be more wealthy."

It can easily be understood how harsh the economic struggle for power becomes when there is also a racial background behind it. But this blind struggle for power and wealth does not represent the whole picture. For certain restrictions may also be needed between two countries in the interests of world peace and justice. Yet in every instance of this kind the restrictions should be made by mutual consent rather than by force.

"Where restrictions", writes Professor Bonn, "are conceived in the spirit of international fairness, when they are not couched in the language of national arrogance, by which a race, doubtful of maintaining its position, is trying to exclude its ablest competitors by branding them as moral inferiors, misunderstanding can be avoided. Friction is due far more to the methods of unfair discrimination, to ebullitions of racial arrogance, and to indecent application of otherwise quite decent laws, than to the mere economic fact of control."

An outstanding example of this was the sudden and sensational passing of the Asiatic Exclusion Act, by the United States in 1924, to which reference has been already made. A result almost exactly similar might have been reached by putting India, China, and Japan on the quota basis. This would not have involved the admission of more than 150 each year from each country. But the actual methods by which this Act was put through converted an economic measure into a racial insult. So deeply was this felt by Oriental people that its unhappy effect remains to the present time.

PART IV

RECOMMENDATIONS AND CONCLUSIONS

In consideration of the evidence that has been brought before the Commission and embodied in this report, the Commission makes the following recommendations:

THE LEAGUE OF NATIONS AND RACIAL EQUALITY

The League of Nations, owing to the threat of the withdrawal of some of its original members, refused to endorse the proposal of Japan that a clause should be inserted in the Preamble of the Covenant of the League declaring racial equality to be a fundamental principle of the League itself.

This action of the League, to which President Wilson submitted under pressure, has been reviewed and considered by a sub-Committee of the Commission. The question of an appeal to the Assembly of the League of Nations, asking for a reconsideration of this vital issue, was discussed by them at length. It was realised during the discussion that trust in the League, as standing impartially for all the nations of the world, was likely to be impaired unless some clear expression of racial equality were placed on record at the very forefront of the Covenant of the League. The objection was raised that the League, in its rules and regulations, dealt with nations, and that equality was recognised among them; but it was pointed out that Article XXIII dealt directly with racial justice and that the principle of racial equality needed clear expression, if the

East was to take its full share in the League's
work.

While it was decided that no direct action,
even in so vital a matter as this, could be taken
by the Commission as such, it was considered that
the Executive of the World Conference for International Peace through Religion might rightly
be asked to take up the subject. The Conference
itself, at one of its sessions, might make a demand
for the recognition of racial equality in all international bodies. It was thought that no single
action would do more to remove at one stroke
grave suspicions and misapprehensions than the
full and unconditional affirmation of racial equality at the very centre of international action.
Such a gesture would serve to remove the com-
plaint seriously uttered by many that international bodies tend in reality to become associated
virtually with the Western Powers in practice,
and that the Eastern peoples are asked to send
their representatives merely for form's sake and
not on a basis of *bona fide* equality.

A Threefold Approach to Racial Justice

The Commission also submits a programme
containing three main lines of approach to the
solution of outstanding racial injustice. They are
as follows:

(*a*) Through a world institution at Geneva
wherein race relations should be an integral
factor.

(*b*) Through the universities and schools.

(*c*) Through the world religious organisations.

The League of Nations itself in its own Covenant (Article XXIII (b)) when grouping together the humanitarian causes of the world, which the League is prepared to uphold, mentions especially as one of these causes, the defence of the weaker races against injustice. The members of the League, who have such races under their political control, pledge themselves in Article XXIII to put an end to such unjust treatment wherever it is pointed out to them by the League.

In spite of this solemn declaration, nothing has been done hitherto to implement this clause concerning racial injustice. Therefore, there appears to be needed at Geneva some voluntary institution supported by world opinion, which might take up this subject along with others whose scope is world-wide and keep the attention of the League turned towards this clause in the Covenant. Such an institution at Geneva, not being under the League but independent of it, might become also a clearing house and centre of reference for those interracial committees and councils which are already working locally in different parts of the world to remove racial friction.

Examples of such local councils and committees are the Interracial Committee established at Atlanta, Georgia, U.S.A., with Dr. Will Alexander as its Secretary; the European and Bantu Joint Councils, at Johannesburg, South Africa, with Dr. Rheinallt Jones as its Secretary; the Joint Council to promote understanding between white and coloured people in Great Britain, with Sir Francis Younghusband as its President and Mr. Henry Polak as Chairman of its Executive Committee; and the Institute of Pacific

Relations at Honolulu. Different bodies such as these and others like them, if they so wished, could become linked up with a world institution at Geneva, which would thus enable them to get into touch with the work that is being done in other parts of the world on the same subject.

The Commission recommends for the consideration of the Executive that:

"It is advisable to establish at Geneva without delay on a voluntary basis an Institute of an international character, which shall have for one of its objects the study of race relations as they affect world peace and the promotion of efforts to reach a solution by removing causes of race friction, and by linking together wherever possible organisations already existing for the same purpose."

While it is not suggested that the World Conference should itself be responsible for establishing such an institution or for any financial obligation connected with it, it is felt that it might assist by giving such a proposal the weight of its moral support.

The second part of the recommendation consists of an appeal to the universities and schools to undertake a thoroughly impartial and scientific study of race relations with a view to reaching some generally accepted conclusions. This would include the anthropological study of race origins, the exploring of the old spiritual heritages of the different races, and such historical and biological research as might throw light on the meaning of "race" and its function in the world. It would also include a scientific outlook on the future of the human race in reference to world population. Different universities in America and Europe are already deeply interested in the international aspect of this subject, and it is likely also that the universities of the East may be willing to co-operate in such research on strictly scientific lines. At the same time, what might be called "laboratory work" could be done by the interracial councils which are engaged in studying racial problems in a practical manner in the local areas most affected.

The third section relates the race problem to the religious organisations of the world for their cordial co-operation and assistance. Two resolutions of primary importance have been adopted unanimously at the Lambeth Conference of 1930, to which Anglican bishops from all over the world assembled. The first of these asserts that no Christian Communicant shall ever be refused access to the Table of the Lord at Holy Communion in any Church solely on the ground of colour or race. The second of these states that where, in any particular area, on account of differences in language and custom the races are normally accustomed to worship apart, special occasions shall be sought from either side for common worship and corporate communion in order to realise the unity of the Body of Christ. It is hoped that similar resolutions will be unanimously passed in other Christian bodies also.

While, in this manner, steps are being taken in the Christian Church, it is noticeable that the religious leaders in other faiths also are already taking action. For instance, the foremost leaders in the Hindu religion are actively engaged in the removal of the racial inequalities, such as "untouchability", which have become wrongly mixed up with traditional practice. On every side it is clear that the time has now come for religion, in its widest sense, to seek to bring about world peace through racial reconciliation, eliminating every traditional custom or teaching that stands in its way, and co-operating with every effort that helps forward the end in view. The World Conference for International Peace through Religion has come at the right time to focus different efforts on a world object and a world purpose.

The Method of Conference for Settling Race Questions

In close connection with these proposals, Dr. Rabindranath Tagore, one of the Presidents of the World Conference, submits the following statement:

"I regard the race and colour prejudice, which barricades human beings against one another, as the greatest evil of modern times which has to be overcome if humanity must be realised as one in spirit. The paths along which progress may be made towards recovery from this evil are manifold. My own stress would be laid upon the elevation of the public mind and the collection and dissemination of accurate scientific knowledge, as against the pseudo-science and pseudo-religion which in their disguise of truth are treacherously dealing mortal blows against Truth herself. There should be a united effort to combine the emotional forces of religion in its broadest sense, with the spread of education based on fully ascertained truth concerning the human race as a whole."

In addition to this general statement, Dr. Tagore further submits a practical suggestion. The most vital need, he asserts, as already pointed out, is research in the universities of the world, and at the centres where the race evil is most apparent. But this research work needs summing up and presenting to the world by unimpeachable authorities. Not merely the Western universities but the Eastern also should be invited to join in the great task, so that the world may be united in its effort to solve this world problem once for all. The best minds of East and West should be brought together. Those whose world opinion stands above current politics should meet and state the case in new terms. He earnestly hopes that the World Conference for International Peace through Religion may do much in helping to bring about such a meeting, and also to mobilise public opinion in this direction.

A new method for dealing with interracial difficulties has clearly to be devised, which shall take the place of the old appeal to arms. The method of conference is required. But the new technique of interracial settlement by conference has to be carefully mapped out; and the fears of the East have to be met before cordial co-operation can be expected. The course that Dr. Tagore proposes, namely, a world opinion expressed by the best minds of East and West, meeting in conference, is likely to fulfil its object, because it stands above all political strife and diplomatic manœuvring. As a Commission, therefore, we would ask for its support and its formal recommendation by the World Conference.

Some action must be taken speedily to restore

confidence and hope in the world. Unless action
is taken from the centre by those who are trusted
and respected, as standing out above racial and
national prejudice, for humanity itself, a further
drifting apart of the races of the world is likely
to happen, and a still wider and more lamentable
estrangement. Therefore, at the present critical
juncture in interracial relations, this Commission
asks the World Conference for International
Peace through Religion to reaffirm in an unmistakable manner the fundamental belief that mankind is one Family, and that the different races
of the world are members together of that one
Family, who should meet and live together on
the basis of mutual equality and respect.

IV

RELIGION AS A CAUSE OF WAR

1. By Henry A. Atkinson

RELIGION is one of the deepest sentiments which control the actions of man, and the religions of the world represent the one interest most nearly universal that affects human life. There are many forms of worship and religious practice, for no tribe has ever been found, even in the most remote parts of the earth, without some kind of religious faith. It is, therefore, one of the most powerful influences we have, and the most far-reaching, for it penetrates to every act of the individual and reaches out to the furthest limits of the community, the state, the nation, the world.

Religion has been, in the past, one of the most fruitful causes of war. It is, and has been, a fighting force. Catholic has been opposed to Protestant, and Protestant to Catholic; Jew and Arab, Hindu and Moslem, Lutheran and Calvinist, Methodist and Baptist—these very names signify opposing forces. Everyone is familiar with the quarrels and difficulties which arise between the various sects, and the long controversies that have been waged over the interpretation of some obscure passage in the Scriptures. The quarrel among Christians

114

themselves makes one of the blackest chapters in
religious history. Europe was torn to pieces for
generations by religious wars. It is difficult to find
a city in Europe that is without some monument
commemorating a victory in one of these wars,
or some building that is connected with a bitter
religious controversy. The hymns of the Church
are saturated with the martial spirit—"Onward,
Christian Soldiers", "The Son of God Goes Forth
to War", "A Mighty Fortress is our God". Crowns
and swords, joustings and fighting are constantly
used as the theme of preachers and theologians.
Jesus, "The Mighty Meek", whose kingdom is
founded upon the Sermon on the Mount, in which
the spirit of non-resistance is the integral part, is
pictured as a martial leader, the captain of the
hosts representing in himself the ancient Hebrew
God of battle.

Not only have wars been fought over religious
subjects and by religious people in behalf of
religious principles, but religion has always played
a part in every war that was ever fought. Kings
and Emperors in the past have ordered prophets
to preach war and priests to bless it. Flags going
out to battle have departed with the benediction
of the Church upon them. Christians on opposing
sides in the Great War prayed each to the same
God for the victory of his arms and the success of
his nation. From 1914 to 1918 the churches were
preaching patriotism in every country and devo-
tion to a common cause. Buying bonds was a
religious ceremony; to die on the battlefield was
to be exalted as a martyr. The Crusades were
made possible by the preaching of an enthusiast
who fired the religious imagination of Europe.

Whole nations and groups of nations, utilising religious sentiment, have plunged into war and heroically sustained the more frightful havoc following war through the religious enthusiasm thus engendered.

By its very definition religion binds man back to l..s God, but in its activities it seems to divide him from his fellow-men. The Fatherhood of God is a doctrine much easier to accept as an article of faith than the universal brotherhood of man, if one is to judge by practical results. Religion has always identified itself with racial and national aspirations. Every war at some period, if it lasted long enough, became a "Holy War". Love, peace, and forbearance are the foundation of every religion; yet to hate one's enemies and love one's friends is the practical basis of all religious faith. Confucius said, "Within the four seas all are brethren", but within the four seas meant within the limits of the Chinese Empire as he knew it. The universalism preached by Jesus brought Him into active opposition with his own people. Religion is always on the side of the "powers that be". Churches of all kinds, everywhere, as expressions of the religious life, are by their very nature conserving factors in the life of the people.

All of this is manifestly true, and can be proved over and over in every country and almost every era of history. However, a deeper study and a truer analysis will convince anyone that there have been very few purely religious wars; that is, wars fought solely for religion and in the interests of religion. The Moslem armies went out ostensibly to convert the Christian world to the Moslem

faith, but behind that movement was the desire
and the determination to build up a great world
empire. It was national aggression using religious
enthusiasm. The Crusades, pictured as a religious
enterprise, were the Holy War *par excellence.*
Christian nations joined forces to rescue the Holy
Sepulchre from the hands of the Saracens, but
behind this religious motive was a deeper one—
the greed of the West, and the belief that a path-
way could be opened up between its capitals and
the great centres of wealth in the Far East. It was
this restless movement that lay at the beginning
of the Renaissance and was behind the great
explorers. It was this that sent adventurers out
to the ends of the earth, and it was this same spirit
that discovered America — religion utilised for
trade and government enterprises, as well as
commercial advantage. Behind the forcible conversion to Christianity of the nations, and the
sword of the conquerors, dripping with the blood
of those who refused to abandon their ancient
faith, was the grim figure of the Emperor who,
through his priests, baptized in the name of
the Father, Son, and Holy Ghost, and took over
new lands in the name of the Imperial Crown.
The Cross erected over the newly built church
matched the flag of the conqueror proudly flying
over the newly built garrison.

The clash between Jew and Arab in Palestine,
and the recent deplorable riots and savage
slaughter are not the result of religious controversy or rivalry. There is no quarrel between the
Arab and his Jewish neighbour. Zionism is not
interested in maintaining the synagogue over
against the mosque; in fact, many of the Zionist

colonies have no synagogue. The Wailing Wall is merely incidental. The clash is between a conquering minority gradually becoming dominant, and a static majority that feels its helplessness in Palestine and its kinship to the larger questions involved in a pan-Arab State. The interests of Arabia, Egypt, Syria, Trans-Jordania, and Iraq are being fought out in Palestine.

Religion, then, it must be conceded, is both a cause for war and a means of fighting wars, and has often been used as a cloak to disguise the real purpose for which people and nations have fought.

In connection with a study of the causes that make for war, one cannot neglect the study of religion in this relationship, and at the same time this question may, with profit, be raised: Can religion, that plays such an important part in human life, be made as strong a factor for peace as it has been for war?

IV—*Continued*

THE HINDU-MUSLIM SITUATION IN INDIA

2. By A. Yusuf Ali

THE Hindu-Muslim differences in India cannot really be classified as among the causes likely to lead to war. They are a feature of the internal, social, and political situation in India. War is a matter between organised States, and not between communities or sections of communities within a single political State.

At the same time, I recognise that Hindu-Muslim differences in creating friction do create that intellectual and social atmosphere which unsettles institutions and bars future progress. If we could imagine the Hindus ever forming a State by themselves, and the Indian Muslims again forming States by themselves, the mental and social differences would undoubtedly lead to collisions. It is, therefore, of some importance to study their causes and consider possible remedies.

Hindu-Muslim differences are not religious differences so much as communal differences. In matters of religion Hinduism itself is an abstraction from a number of ideas and doctrines, often irreconcilable, which have not been embodied into a system by any authoritative organisation.

119

In so far as there is any historical or psychological unity, that unity fits in well with the general Eastern attitude of religion to ideas of Nature, God, and the Universe. Islam has definite religious, social, political, and moral ideas which have been embodied in a system authoritatively expounded in books and in the lives of leaders, which are accepted as patterns or guides for individual life. Though there are sects and differences, there is enough body of common ideas and doctrines which can be labelled under the general name of Islam to give scope for a definite and consistent presentment. It will be found, however, that such a presentment again fits in well with the large ideas common to all religions of the East. In this way Hinduism and Islam, in their basic ideas, subject to what we have said already, are not necessarily antagonistic. Many of the Sufi writings breathe the same speculative atmosphere as the Upanishads and the Vedas. Maulana Jalal-ud-dim Rumi's poetry belongs to the same mystic type as that of Doctor Rabindranath Tagore. The attitude of mind in both is born of a realisation that the human spirit is one, and that its unity is caused by its kinship with the Divine. It is realised that the only ultimate reality is the existence of God. The reality of phenomena is merely apparent or temporary. In religious ideas themselves there need be, and is, no conflict. The conflict in practical life comes from other causes.

The communal conflicts as between Hindus and Muslims in India are very real. They are like the hard knots in wood, which a cabinetmaker finds so difficult to smooth out and polish. The communal differences, although they can be reconciled, yet stand out as snags in the smooth navigation of the ship of constitutional progress. Their causes are partly historical, partly racial, partly temperamental, and partly social.

Psycho-analysts tell us that the sub-conscious elements in the history of an individual are more important even than the conscious elements. This truth is particularly applicable to the Hindu-Muslim communities. That takes us to the whole history of India for the last ten centuries. The outstanding facts of that history are fairly clear and have been frequently investigated, but they are by no means admitted on all sides. But the interpretations to be placed on those facts is not at all clear and gives rise to very violent controversies. That is the reason why no standard history of India during that period has been written or can be written until the communal atmosphere is cleared. But whatever the causes for the easy establishment of Muslim political supremacy in India may have been, the fact remains that until the middle of the eighteenth century the Muslims had undisputed supremacy over the whole peninsula of India. This supremacy was mainly political, but political supremacy reacted on social life and on thoughts and ideas. It even affected the languages of India, and gave birth to that wonder among the modern vernaculars of India, the Urdu language and literature. Even after the middle of the eighteenth century until, say, the middle of the nineteenth century, while the political supremacy of the Muslims faded gradually, and the political supremacy of the British ideas and institutions gained ground, the Muslim law remained in the background as a sort of common law of India, and Muslim prestige continued to operate in various directions. The Indian Muslims find it difficult to readjust their focus under the new conditions, in which they have not only lost political supremacy, but they are threatened with an assault on the cultural ideas which they cherish, and on the unity of structure in their social life.

Racially, 80 per cent or 90 per cent of the Indian Muslims belong to ethnic stocks similar to those of their Hindu brethren in the different areas of India. But the foreign element—Arab, Persian, Afghan, Turk, or Mughal—formed the governing class in the days of Muslim rule, and they created a new social atmosphere for the Muslim community as a whole. Race is not recognised in Islam as a ground of differentiation or distinction, and intermarriage among the Muslims has tended to bring some homogenity into the Muslim social fabric, though complete homogenity has not yet been achieved. But a democratic social system without caste, and the freedom from child marriage, and the liberty of widow remarriage, have tended, on the whole, to strengthen the numerical proportion of Muslims in the population, while meat and more varied diet have preserved or improved their physique compared with that of their vegetarian Hindu brethren. For these reasons, sometimes, the Muslims are spoken of as a separate race, and prejudices and sympathies, akin to those that arise from racial differentiation, have tended to make themselves felt as between Hindu and Muslim communities.

This may to a certain extent account for tem-

peramental differences. For there is no doubt
that such do exist. They are the hardest to tackle
or to remedy. The Rajputs and the Jats get on
well with the Muslims, but the commercial and
money-lending classes (mainly Hindu) are repugnant to the martial, or administrative, or
agricultural classes among the Muslims, in the
same way that the Jews are repugnant to the
Christian population among whom they live.
Usually the Jews are in a minority among Christian populations. In India, in most provinces, the
Muslims are in a minority. It is the fate of most
minorities to suffer, but this minority suffering
accentuates the temperamental repugnance between the two communities.

The social differences have been referred to,
but it would be well to examine them more closely.
The whole structure of Hindu society is based on
caste. The whole basis of Muslim society is social
and religious equality. Such a society in the midst
of a caste-ridden society is treated as if it were
itself a new caste. And the position of castelessness becomes almost a mark of inferiority.
Castelessness, instead of being a merit, as it would
be where it dominated, becomes a reproach, as if
it were equivalent to being out-casted. It is true
that the bonds of caste are being relaxed by
modern movements in Hinduism, and more attention is being given to "untouchables", but the
Muslim position is that condescending attention
to "untouchables" is a different thing from the
frank recognition of social equality and equality
of opportunities. Some friction is caused by religious conversions which bring the "untouchables" at once into a brotherhood of equality,

instead of being patronised by movements of "uplift" and similar fine-sounding names.

The result of all this clash of sentiment and history is that the two communities have collectively little confidence in each other. In the modern political reforms, therefore, the Muslims insist on separate electorates, which do not tend to heal the breach. Other minorities are also coming forward, claiming separate treatment. Separate communal schools and colleges are also springing up. Communal riots sometimes arise because of the slaughter of cows for food, the cow being a sacred animal to the Hindus. When feelings are inflamed, the communities come into collision over religious processions or the beating of tom-toms before mosques.

No heroic remedies are possible where the feelings are so deep-seated. The radical remedy is the cultivation of the true religious spirit, which must mean, both for Muslims and Hindus, ideas of fair play, respect for other people's feelings, reverence for other people's religious ideas, and toleration for other people's rites and ceremonies. But this, in order to be effective, should be mutual. The study of each other's literatures and ideas may be helpful. A greater feeling of common responsibility and common citizenship in the new political future opening out before India may also do much to turn the attention of the masses to matters of common interest. Association with other nations and peoples who have solved similar difficulties by the exercise of good sense and a feeling of human solidarity would also be an important factor. Every influence tending to human solidarity must be used. I consider, therefore, that

the methods and example of the World Conference for International Peace through Religion
may, by reflex action, exert a salutary influence
on this, the most intricate of our domestic
problems in India.

V

SCIENCE AND WAR

By Sir J. Arthur Thomson

How the Authority and Approbation of Science may be falsely invoked as an Influence that makes for War

No council of judges would allow a hearing of the accusation that science sometimes favours war, for science is primarily concerned with making things intelligible; and no increase of understanding can possibly make for war. So it is necessary to modify the indictment, and ask how science or mistaken science may be used by those who would make war—who have been skilful enough sometimes to make even religion play into their hands.

It is necessary to draw a distinction between discovery which makes the world more translucent and must always be in the line of progress, and practical invention which may be outrageously used for evil purposes. But science is hardly to be blamed for the abuse of its discoveries by inventors.

To what are we referring? To what has become

the familiar reproach that modern science supplies those dire sinews that have made war so
terrifically destructive. We refer to the tremendous explosives, the big guns, the planes and air-
ships that drop bombs, the insidious submarines
(that blow up *Lusitanias*), and so on through the
list of devilishly ingenious and effective contriv-
ances.

Some thinkers have been so horrified that they
have asked whether science deserves any longer
to be fostered. But this is an idle question, since
science will continue to be subsidised as long
as it increases man's mastery of Nature, which
spells wealth and luxuries, freedom and fullness
of life, as well as engines of destruction, and a
flood of ugliness. Furthermore, science is ir-
repressible, for even if the inquisitive spirit is
starved, it will continue to make discoveries. So
there is no use in saying that science must stop
because inventions have been so destructive. It
is conceivable, however, that a highly moralised
discoverer might, in certain cases, repress his
invention because he thought that civilisation
was not ready for it.

How then are we to answer the reproach that
science has made war tenfold more terrible than
ever? There is a crumb of comfort in the fact
that a new thrust evokes a new parry, as when
a counteractive is found for a poison-gas. Only
a crumb of comfort, however, for a still subtler
poison is then invented, a still bigger gun, a still
more powerful explosive. But if this line of
thought is pursued, it leads to the suggestion
that the increased deadliness of the weapons will
eventually make war impossible. The weapons

may become too sharp to be handled with safety.
The engines of war may become so unthinkably
terrible that they will be consigned to the scrap
heap by the common consent of the nations, and
other solutions will evolve.

In the strict sense, of course, it is not science
as such that is to blame, but our imperfect
human nature that uses knowledge for evil purposes. There is no ethical note in the discovery
of a more powerful explosive than the world has
yet known; it might be used for laudable geo-
technic purposes. The ethical note is sounded
when man uses this new force for the wholesale
destruction of his fellow-creatures. In the same
way it is neither right nor wrong to discover a
new poison. For this might prove an invaluable
medicine; and there is no ethical issue until the
newly discovered power begins to be used; it may
be used to save life, it may be used to destroy.

The indictment of "science" as an influence
supporting war must be met by the question,
What Science? For if the "science" be a world-out-
look that denies any uniqueness in living beings,
that denies the reality of mind as a *vera causa*
in the life and evolution of the higher animals,
that denies that man is more than a mammal,
and human society more than a herd, then what
such a "science" says is to be distrusted down to
the ground, and what it supports must be evil.

When people invoke the authority of science
as supporting the theory that wars are necessary
for the progress of civilisation, one must inquire
whether the scientific conclusions invoked are

accepted by all competent authorities. Science
ought to be quite impersonal and verifiable, but,
in the less exact sciences especially, there is, in
the wake of what is certain, a wash of opinion;
and the expression given to a scientific conclusion
is often coloured by the metaphysics or prejudices of the expositor. Thus we are not influenced by any apologies for warfare that come
from exclusively mechanistic biology, or from
dogmatic apsychic ecology, or from extreme be-
haviourism that declares mind to be a mere
foam-bubble epiphenomenon, or from a bio-
logistic sociology that regards a society as a mere
herd; for as scientific inquirers we are convinced
that the views we have referred to are all
erroneous, not to say superstitious. Apart from
Einsteinian subsuming, there is unanimity in including the Law of Gravitation as a certainty for
the order of facts in regard to which it was
formulated, but can anyone say the same for
the mechanistic formulation of a dog or a man?
But we can imagine that those who profess to
regard biology as a rather recondite branch of
hydrodynamics will give their support to war as
readily as to cricket.

Speaking for ourselves, of course, we think
there is considerable evidence in support of the
view that the Conflict of Races has had some
useful influence in the evolution of civilisation.
We have had, in a busy life, no opportunity of
investigating this theory, but we had the advantage of many long talks with the late Mr.
Stuart-Glennie, a learned protagonist of that pro-
war sociological doctrine. But we would suggest

K

that, since civilisation has evolved and is evolving, there is good reason to ask whether methods of sifting which worked not wholly for evil in the past—since *we* are here—may not have entirely outlived their usefulness. There is some basis for the saying *Lupus lupo lupus*, "a wolf a wolf to other wolves"; but to generalise this for mankind—*Homo homini lupus*—is a superstition.

There is one other consideration that we wish to submit. We are jealous of the reputation of science as a disinterested attempt to make the world, and man's share in it, more intelligible; and so we have maintained (1) that discovery is not to blame for the abuse of inventions based on it; (2) that if an appeal is made to science, it must be to the science of living beings as well as to the science of things and forces, and to the science of societies as well as to biology; (3) that established science is not to be blamed for the penumbra of opinion around unsolved problems, nor for the admixture of prejudice and metaphysics that is apt to be involved in the exposition of conclusions arrived at in the less exact fields; and (4) that mistakes are made by science, which are apt to be seized upon by those who seek for "good reasons" for their reversionary promptings. But our final suggestion is just this: that scientific conclusions at their best are partial and abstract; they are accurate and reliable, but only *towards* truth. Their partiality and abstractness must be corrected, if need be, by the results of following *other* pathways towards reality. And here we are content to leave the question of the legitimacy of aggressive warfare.

VI

THE CULTURAL CAUSES OF WAR

By Alfred Zimmern

THE title assigned to this study is, of course, deliberately paradoxical. Culture and warfare might seem at first sight to stand in no relation whatsoever the one to the other. Intrinsically indeed they are not even at opposite poles: they are in different worlds. Culture, however we define that elusive conception, is an attribute of the individual: war is a relationship of conflict between states or political societies. Moreover, on the plane of individual life, culture is an element making for grace, proportion, and harmony in the human spirit: so far from causing conflicts in the mind or the soul, its characteristic function is to act as a moderating and assuaging influence. Conflict indeed, and what may be by analogy termed warfare, are necessary for the development of the human spirit—for all men at some time and for some men almost continuously. But if any criticism is to be levelled at the ideal and the processes of culture it is surely just this—that they may tend to fix men unduly in stereotyped ways of thinking and feeling, ministering to a self-satisfaction which inhibits

initiative rather than stimulating them to fresh
efforts with all the possible conflicts involved.
Does not the term culture call up to us those
essays of Matthew Arnold in which, with an
almost uncultural insistence, he emphasises its
qualities of "sweetness and light"? Or Browning's
Old Pictures in Florence in which he contrasts
culture, in the form of the Hellenic ideal of perfection, with the ideal of eternal growth, effort
and struggle which inspires Christian art from
Giotto onwards?

> Are they perfect of lineament, perfect of stature?
>   In both, of such lower types are we
> Precisely because of our wider nature;
>   For time, theirs—ours, for eternity.
> To-day's brief passion limits their range;
>   It seethes with the morrow for us and more.
> They are perfect—how else? they shall never change:
>   We are faulty—why not? we have time in store.
> The Artificer's hand is not arrested
>   With us; we are rough-hewn, no-wise polished:
> They stand for our copy, and, once invested
>   With all they can teach, we shall see them abolished.

And does not the contrast between the
"rough-hewn" and the "polished" summon back
to our minds the memorable description in
Renan's *St. Paul* of those models of classical
culture, the Athenian professors, to whom the
apostle addressed in vain the Word of Life?
"Athens, at the point to which it has been brought
after centuries of development, a city of gram-
marians, of gymnasts and of teachers of sword-
play, was as ill-disposed as possible to receive
Christianity. The banality and inward dryness
of the schoolman are irremediable sins in the eyes
of grace. The pedagogue is the most difficult of

men to convert: for he has his own religion, which consists in his routine, his faith in his old authors, his taste for literary exercises: this contents him and extinguishes every other need. There has been discovered at Athens a series of portrait-busts of university dignitaries of the second century A.D. They are handsome figures, grave and imposing, with a noble air which is still Hellenic. The inscriptions record for us the honour and pensions which they enjoyed: the real great men of the older democracy never received so much. Assuredly, if St. Paul encountered any of the predecessors of these splendid pedants, he must have met with no more success than a neo-Catholic romantic at the time of the Empire would have had with an academic devotee of Horace, or, in our own day, a humanitarian socialist, inveighing against British prejudice, with the Fellows of Oxford or Cambridge."

Here we come upon a possible relationship between culture and warfare—namely, that culture, being essentially static, exposes itself to the risk of being swept away by the dynamic force of change or "progress" which may manifest itself in the form of organised warfare. But, whatever verdict we may pass on wars of this kind, of which the struggles attending the decline and fall of the Roman Empire may be taken as an example, it is only in a very negative sense that culture can be described as their cause. The initiative in the conflict comes, in such cases, not from the cultured but from the uncultured, and the war is undertaken, not in the name of culture or of civilisation, but, if any justifying watchword is needed at all, of poverty against riches, of freedom against privilege or of virility against senescence. Culture is here not the assailant but the defender, and a defender, moreover, who, in spite of the teachers of sword-play in the vicinity, has a natural predilection for the reasonable processes of compromise and arbitration as against more summary decisions by force of arms.

But in seeking for the cultural causes of war we are not concerned with the causes which may lead the uncultured into disputes and then into warfare with the cultured. These, predominantly economic in character as they are, have no doubt been duly analysed in their appropriate place. What we are concerned with here is causes of war in which culture is involved on the side of the assailant. Since, as we have seen, culture is an individual quality of a peculiarly peaceable kind, and not therefore a political force making for aggression, we shall clearly not succeed in identifying it as a cause of war, in the natural sense of the word "cause": *i.e.* as an "efficient or promoting activity". The same may be said of religion, which, though less harmonious in its working within the human spirit, certainly never launched an ultimatum or set a battle in array. The saint may be a less congenial member of society than the scholar-gentleman of Renan's portrait-busts, but his eyes are fixed on the heavens and not on some earthly end to be attained by the clash of arms. Yet we are perfectly familiar with the idea of "wars of religion". And, on reflection, we realise that these have not been wars waged by saints for saintly ends, whether for individual salvation through good works

or for the salvation of the souls of the enemy
people, but have been conflicts in which the name
and cause of religion have been invoked for purposes quite extraneous to religion in its pure and
proper sense as a quality or attitude of the individual soul involving a relationship between
the soul and God. Exactly in the same way,
culture, also a quality of the individual, has been
used as a cover for political action, its essential
qualities of harmony and reasonableness being
all the more useful by contrast for the work for
which its name and authority are borrowed and
prostituted. It is therefore culture as an *occasion*
rather than as a *cause* of war with which we shall
be concerned.

It may be convenient to begin by stating the
problem in its sharpest terms.

Among the products of the potter's art which
bear the unmistakable mark of Greek culture,
in all its grace, simplicity, and dignity, there are
a number which reveal, through the signature
of their artificers, that they have been fashioned
by the fingers of slaves. Here we are faced, in the
most direct manner, with the problem of culture
as a justification for the use of violence. A boy
from the Northern Balkans or from the interior
of Asia Minor or of North Africa is torn from his
surroundings, packed on a ship, exposed in a
slave-market and acquired as an apprentice for
an Athenian potter's workshop. Within a few
years, under the influence of his new surroundings and the impression of their prestige, he has
ceased to be a barbarian, a dead piece of foreign
workshop equipment, and has become a junior
member of the household, assimilated into its

culture, and even sharing in its creativeness. And the adjustment, if peaceable in its later stages, has been effected by violence, through the operation of that slave-trade which is so much more repugnant to Christian sentiment than normal warfare that it was abolished by international agreement a hundred years before the establishment of a League of Nations.

To an enlightened fifth-century Athenian, emancipated from traditional conceptions of race or clan or local worship, such slave signatures would have been a matter for unquestioning satisfaction. They would have been considered as a vindication in themselves of the educational process that they reveal. Such an Athenian would have seen in them a proof, firstly that the forcible assimilation of members of an inferior culture into a superior could be carried through with complete success, and secondly that it was not only practicable but desirable, in the interests of the world as a whole, and not least in those of the inferior peoples. Athens was the schoolmaster not only of Hellas but of the world. Her school was admittedly not simply first-rate but unique. Why should she not adopt compulsory methods of attendance, employing violence if necessary to draw in her students from the highways and hedges?

"Compel them to come in." Such has been the argument of organised benevolence, whether in the sphere of education, or of colonial government, or of social policy, or even sometimes of religion, throughout the ages. The Athenian slave-master justified his acquiescence in the slave-trade because through it his Thracian and his

Lydian found a gateway to the appreciation of the real values of life. Modern imperialism, in the interests of the same civilisation, has constantly resorted to violence and warfare in order to replace primitive by more modern and effective forms of government and administration. And within our own western industrial communities compulsion has become a recognised instrument of social policy in establishing new habits and standards of living and in assimilating backward portions of the community into the larger central mass. And in certain countries, at a time when religious orthodoxy held the place in men's scale of values which culture held in fifth-century Athens, force of the same kind was employed, even to the extremest penalty of the law, not for the object of elevating men's culture or modernising their institutions or improving their social habits, but of saving their souls. If culture, in the shape of the Athenian slave-master, held a lash in reserve for a recalcitrant apprentice, religion, in a particular variety of Spanish Catholicism, could enforce its teaching by the fire and the stake.

We see then what our problem is. *Culture becomes a cause of war when the representatives of a superior culture, possessing also superior power, employ that power to impose their culture upon an inferior party.* But we see also that our problem, thus stated, involves a far wider issue than that of the clash of cultures in warfare. Can we draw an absolute distinction between one particular form of pressure, through organised warfare, and the various other forms of pressure involved in the relationship between superior and inferior

cultures? And if we justify warfare as a means
for rescuing savage communities from the
arbitrary domination of tribal chiefs, we have to
face the Athenian's, and the old Southerner's,
arguments on behalf of slavery. If Alexander was
justified in annexing Asia Minor in order to
Hellenise it, why are the Greeks of an earlier
generation to be condemned for carrying over
isolated Asiatics to school in Greece? And if, on
the other hand, we condemn resort to violence
as a means for putting an end to the barbarism
of inferior cultures, shall we also not be driven
to question forms of compulsion, even though
they involve no bloodshed, through which entire
social groups and sometimes whole societies are
ruthlessly and mechanically extinguished by
process of law?

Thus analysed, our problem becomes one of
degree. At the two ends of the scale the modern
conscience gives a clear reply. Slavery and the
slave-trade, whatever the educational benefits
which they may result in conferring, stand condemned. (At a recent discussion on forced labour
in the Sixth Commission of the League of Nations
a proposal by the representatives of a colonial
power to allow certain forms of forced labour
because of their educational value fell upon deaf
ears.) On the other hand, modern opinion has
moved, and is still moving, towards more and
more extensive approval of measures of social
compulsion even when they do violence to individual tastes, temperaments, and inclinations.
The greatest good of the greatest number is held
to justify a large measure of individual sacrifice
and subordination. The problem arises in the

intermediate region, in the whole range of issues involved by the contact between superior and inferior cultures.

Is the superior culture, when it is also superior in physical power, justified in intervening by force in putting down evil practices and rescuing the oppressed? Until recent years the answer of the immense majority of enlightened opinion in Britain, if not in America, would undoubtedly have been in the affirmative. Men would have pointed to the unquestionable improvement effected by the extension of the rule of the British and other governments, by the employment or the threat of force, over vast areas in Asia, Africa, and the South Seas, and would have appealed for inspiration to the robust philosophy of "the White Man's Burden". To-day the situation has changed—for three reasons: firstly, we are no longer so sure that an individual government is the best judge of the advisability of the resort to force in the interests of civilisation; secondly, men are less confident than they were in the absolute validity of the distinction between "superior" and "inferior" cultures, and in the representative character of the members of the "superior" culture who enter into contact with the inferior, sometimes for purposes of private profit; thirdly, since the whole habitable globe has been divided up into political jurisdictions the days of what may be called pioneering, or even buccaneering, philanthropy are over, and all government action of this kind clearly concerns, not merely the two parties concerned, but the whole international community.

We can say, then, that the resort to war by an

individual Government, even against a slave-power whose barbarous practices are clearly proved and admitted, is no longer to be held justifiable. It is for the international community to lay down general rules, forbidding slavery and other indefensible social practices, and to enforce such rules by appropriate means. In other words, the vague terms "superior" and "inferior" should be replaced by a definite list of practices which are so clearly "inferior" that, like illiteracy in Western Europe, they are destined to be abolished by governmental action.

If we admit this principle, which we may define as *the principle of International Cultural Minimum*, we shall find it easier to face the problem involved in the use of forms of compulsion falling short of actual warfare or violence. For in condemning this or that specific practice our principle implicitly refuses to make a distinction between cultures as such: still more emphatically, by asserting the doctrine of equality before the law, does it rule out the idea that there is any necessary relationship between superior power and culture.

What indeed is a superior culture? If, as was suggested above, culture is a quality of the individual rather than of a group, the phrase is, strictly speaking, meaningless: social institutions which in one generation may show to their credit the most admirable specimens of humanity may a generation or two later be a mere breeding-ground for degenerates. The noble savage of one age may be the refuse of the next. We cannot speak of Russian culture being superior to Red Indian or British to Masai till we know what sort

of individuals are predominant or typical in each
of those communities. But, leaving aside the
question of words, a superior culture may
roughly be defined as a culture tending to produce a type of individual who has a cultured
personality. And when we examine the complex
elements which go to the making of such a personality we find that one of the most essential is
a sense of personal freedom, dignity, and self-
respect. Now this is precisely the quality which
is automatically destroyed by the institution of
slavery—and not only by slavery but by any
badge or general recognition of inferiority of
status. Thus we arrive at the conclusion that,
except in the rare cases of personalities powerful
enough to counteract the pervading influence of
their social environment, a "culture" or social
group recognised as inferior will not produce cultured individuals, or, at least, that it will tend
to produce individuals lacking in one of the essential elements of culture. Thus the term "inferior
culture" is shown to be a misnomer, for in so far
as there is recognised inferiority the door is practically closed to true culture. The same argument
may be applied to the term "superior culture",
for the sense of group or class superiority, such
as existed among societies of slave-holders,
though it has exhibited graces of its own in the
past, is surely a severe drawback to the development in the individual of the humane and harmonious quality which is almost as essential as
liberty itself to the modern idea of culture.

It is suggested then that the right starting-
point for the modern conscience in dealing with
our problem is the acceptance of the principle

that, just as all men are equal in the sight of
God, so all cultures are equal in the international community: all are entitled to equal
consideration: the members of all are entitled
to equal respect. Every culture and every social
group manifest shortcomings and abuses. These
are to be put down by law, by the application
of the International Minimum laid down by an
international authority acting on behalf of the
community of nations. But this code will not
apply simply to the so-called "inferior"—the
backward and primitive and physically weak. It
will apply—it does apply—equally to the strong.
The same authority which last year drew up the
Convention on Forced Labour, with special reference to African conditions, has drawn up other
conventions embodying the stringent regulation
of certain abuses prevalent in industrial Europe
but unknown in Africa. The principle of equality
of cultures before the law rescues the so-called
inferior from the domain of philanthropy and
sets them side by side with their equals in the
realm of international social policy. And in so
doing it deals a shrewd blow at the inferiority and
superiority complexes which are the most fruitful cause of that irritation which, if it no longer
so frequently leads to open conflicts, nevertheless causes the persistence of a kind of suppressed
state of warfare which is the most powerful
obstacle to any real understanding between the
representatives of the cultures concerned.

Once the principle of equality before the law
for the enforcement of an International Minimum
is recognised, our problem is reduced within
manageable proportions. We are not asked to

furnish judgments of value as between one culture and another—between Welsh and English or
Czech and German or Hindu and Moslem or
Malayan and Chinese. We accept each at its own
valuation believing that, in the sphere of culture
as of religion, a personal judgment, however
humble the individual, is preferable to a public
edict. The duty of the public authority is limited,
on the one hand, to keeping watch over the
observance of the minimum, and on the other, to
promoting, by such means as it has at its disposal
the development, in the community as a whole
and among individuals, of those elements of culture which are common to all human beings,
of which self-respect and personal dignity are
among the most important. In a community
governed on these lines conflicts of culture will
be unknown: for such conflicts, of which Europe
and North America afford so many unhappy examples, are manifestations, not of culture allowed
to expand and flower in the open air of a free
community, but of its persecution, suppression,
and consequent politicisation. The most typical
example of such politicisation is, of course, the
Nation-State, which, by branding culture with
a sovereign hall-mark, has dragged it from its
privacy and made it a potent cause of international discord. There could be no more striking
example of the evil results of intellectual confusion in the field of public affairs. To make
participation in a particular culture the criterion
of membership of a State is to destroy the meaning of law, the glory of which is to be common to
men as men, and to obliterate the distinction
between public and private, between the realm of

Caesar and the realm of the spirit. A culture thus erected into a position of political power debases itself for the sake of its own predominance: in seeking to diffuse itself it destroys the very reason of its existence. Where the Nation-State philosophy is accepted, conflicts of culture are inevitable, and it is equally inevitable that they should be decided according to the preponderance of political power, irrespective of the intrinsic character of the cultures concerned. Here no minority treaties or other safeguards will avail, for where fanaticism is afoot in relations between individuals, legal remedies are of little use. The only remedy for such conflicts is to get rid of the confusion and falsehood out of which they spring. Men must learn, in Europe as elsewhere, to think of the State as an organisation transcending and ignoring the idiosyncrasies of this or that social group in its effort to provide the means of good living for them all. They must learn to think of law as the agent, not of the decrees of a particular set of rulers who happen to occupy the seats of power, but of the intelligence, will, and conscience of diverse and miscellaneous human beings united in a community and in social service for the public good. And they must come to realise that, if the waging of war in the name of religion is the darkest stain on the pages of the Christian record, the superiority-complex which invokes the name of culture in its service, whether for open warfare or for secret humiliation, is a sin comparable to that of those of whom it was said that it were better that a millstone were hanged about their neck and that they were drowned in the depth of the sea.

VII

THE PRESS AND WORLD PEACE

By Frederick J. Libby

In considering the relation of the Press to the problem of peace and war it is necessary to distinguish between the possible influence of a consciously united and directed effort on the part of the Press itself, and the influence which at present is exerted, or which can be exerted, through the Press as now organised and controlled.

It is also important to recognise the different fields of influence of three kinds of material: news reports, articles signed by special correspondents, and editorials.

There is no question that if the owners and editors and reporters of the Press of the world decided to use their power to establish peace they could do it. But this assumes a unified purpose and a central control which exists only when Governments direct the Press, as in times of war, or under such dictatorships as those existing to-day in Italy and Russia. Under earlier conditions influential papers did exercise a leadership which, in England for instance, gave the Press credit for achieving Catholic emancipation, the suppression of the slave trade, and the adoption of a policy of free trade. Powerful individual papers have also been the decisive influence on different occasions in actually bringing about a war and in preventing wars. The Spanish-American War has been called a newspaper war, while the outcome of the tense situation between the United States and Mexico affords an instance of the power of the Press successfully exerted for peace. On an earlier occasion war is said to have been averted by the action of a single paper, when, in 1875, the London *Times* published a letter from its Paris correspondent setting forth the facts of the European situation and the preparation for war between Germany and France, which was credited with having stopped hostilities. In his letter of praise to the correspondent, the famous editor of the *Times*, Delane, wrote him: "No greater honour than to have averted war is within the reach of the journalist".

Since the World War there have been several instances of individual papers originating peace measures, or supporting national policies conducive to peace. For example, the *New York World*, immediately after the War, originated a campaign for a disarmament conference, which resulted in the Washington Conference for the Limitation of Armaments. During the 1930–31 World Court campaign a survey showed that out of 2036 papers over two-thirds were in favour of American adherence to the Court.

Nevertheless, it is difficult to see how it can be the function of the Press, as a whole, to assume the task of directing and educating public opinion for a fundamental change in public policy. To do this would mean bending the news columns as well as the editorial columns to a given purpose. The great problem to-day is how to gather from all parts of the earth the facts that it is necessary to have in hand if public policies are to be intelligently determined. The Press attempts to fulfil this function of world-wide fact-gathering. The extreme difficulty of the task is too little appreciated, and the conditions under which it must be performed explain, to a large extent, the character of the Press. Daily news reports hastily gathered are bound to reflect, much as would a daily snapshot, what the world is, not what it is thinking it would like to be, or even what it is tending to become. It is what emerges to the surface of life in the form of startling events. And, so long as the Press must appeal to large numbers of people, these events are bound to be described in terms which will be most easily understood— which is to say, in terms of old or already familiar ideas and ideals, and of universal—therefore primitive—emotions. News columns should be accepted for what they are, and if important phases of life are not adequately reflected in them, then these phases should receive new emphasis and should find new forms of expression.

There is, however, a new method of presenting news which needs special consideration. News columns to-day include articles, signed by special correspondents, which provide more than the bare recital of facts and which actually interpret the news and add to it what amounts to editorial comment. In a recent lecture before Yale University, S. K. Ratcliffe, British journalist, declared the special correspondent to be the most important personage in the newspaper field, with power to change the course of world history. There are two noticeable tendencies among such special correspondents which have been frequently commented upon. One is towards the development of what has been called the international journalist, men who are familiar with many capitals, and with the statesmen of many countries, and who regularly attend the great international conferences and annual meetings of the League of Nations, and thus acquire the habit of seeking their news from the representatives of various Governments, and of presenting news from a world point of view. The other tendency, which is to be found among special correspondents assigned to their home Governments, is one which has developed since the war and out of war conditions. During the war Governments spoke through the newspapers to the people, the Press gave up its function of criticising, even of reporting, and correspondents became in reality ambassadors to the people, helping to carry out national policies. The older relationship of Press and Government has never been fully restored. Departmental publicity bureaux, hand-outs, regular weekly or semi-weekly conferences with the President and Cabinet officers, have continued; and newspaper men, although with a growing number of exceptions, continue to hand out to the public what Government officials hand out to them.

At present there are many special correspondents who definitely seek to make their influence tell on the side of better international understanding and more wholesome international relations. However, no way has so far been devised to insure seriousness of purpose, intelligence, and fair - mindedness in these men who have such power over world events, nor has any way been devised to protect these correspondents against false information, or a misleading reticence as to facts on the part of Government officials. The presence in all capitals of many correspondents does serve, it is true, as a check on notably biased reports, for such reports would promptly lose a journalist his professional standing among his colleagues; while the world-wide honour accorded a man like Walter Duranty, Russian correspondent for the *New York Times*, shows the reward that awaits the consistently well-informed and conscientious writer. But whatever safeguards are placed about their reports, the interpretations offered in special news articles should be accepted with much the same allowance that would be made for possible personal bias in books or other works of individual writers.

The news, strictly speaking, should be watched for three things: the kind of dispatches which are being printed about other countries, the point of view from which the news of Government policies affecting international affairs is presented, and the relative emphasis given to war measures and to peace measures.

The amount of news published about other countries is steadily increasing. There is also more foreign news of a constructive nature dealing with political situations, Government policies, and economic conditions. However, a large amount of foreign news is still of the sensational variety, and affords no true picture of the countries from which it comes. This is, at least in part, due to the fact that news gathered rapidly and designed for the consumption of large numbers of readers must be "salient news" dealing with the common passions of mankind. One influence which may tend to eliminate or reduce sensational personal news from foreign countries is to be found in international Press conferences such as have been held during recent years in Geneva and among Pan-American journalists. Newspaper-men themselves are forming world organisations representing a growing world interest and sense of world responsibility. The International Federation of Journalists is attempting to establish an International Court of Honour, the purpose of which is to prevent the publication of distorted facts, and to hold the individual journalist responsible for the information he sends to his paper. So far as readers are concerned, a campaign such as was carried on by a Church group in the United States would also go far towards correcting news giving a false impression of another country. The Church body referred to organised committees, or secured individual correspondents, in every community; all papers were watched and no news story or editorial comment reflecting unfairly upon the religious belief of the group was allowed to pass unchallenged.

In a definite effort to insure more intelligent handling of the news or a more sympathetic attitude toward other peoples, several European Governments provide travelling scholarships for journalists to enable them to study foreign countries. In the United States opportunities for foreign travel have been afforded to a limited number of editors by the Carnegie Endowment

for International Peace, and through the English-
Speaking Union, which arranges each year for exchange of British and American correspondents.

So far as national policies are concerned, the
news stories on the recent tariff legislation in the
United States and its effect abroad showed a new
tendency to see national policies from a point of
view other than the purely nationalistic, or, even
better, they showed a growing realisation of the
need to take into account present world interdependence in determining national policies. It
is on this ground—that the nationalistic point of
view no longer affords a true reflection of the
world situation—that the Press can be appealed
to, and expected to avoid undue nationalism in
its reports. This is, however, an instance of the
wider appeal to old ideals as compared with new;
and it is not to be expected that the Press will
be entirely free from the out-of-date appeal to
selfish nationalistic sentiments until the public
itself outgrows them, and efforts must be made
through other channels than the Press to educate
the public to understand the relation which
exists to-day between the individual country and
the rest of the world.

As for the emphasis in the news on forces
making for war and on those making for peace, it
is to be remembered that, in any attempt to change
from an old order to a new, those things which
belonged to the old are institutionalised and
active, while in general the forces that are building up the new order are unorganised, and so far
without power to act. The old are also naturally
readily understood by the average reader; the
new are not. In this particular case the war

machine ramifies into every section of the country and into every phase of national life. It has
long been its business to be picturesque news.
When it speaks, it speaks as a part of the Government, and what any Government official says is
news, since there is behind him the power to act.

There is no agency within the Government
created to act in the interest of peace or to serve
as a spokesman for the forces desiring peace.
The State Department might assume this rôle,
but so far has not. No consistent official effort is
being made to educate the public as to the necessity of peace, or as to the various methods proposed to achieve peace as, for instance, Mr.
Hugh Gibson has said it must be educated if
the World Disarmament Conference is to succeed.

This reflection in the Press of an old order,
necessarily strengthening that old order, is a
serious handicap and danger when the essential
thing for progress is to change men's general
conceptions of the world. It is John Morley, in
his *Essay on Compromise*, who says that the
history of civilisation is a history of the replace-
ment of one conception by another more nearly
in accord with the facts. If this is true, it is of the
utmost importance that the new facts of world life
which necessitate world peace should be known.

The situation in Washington is of special importance because of the present dominant position of the United States in world affairs. Every
Government department has its Press section, but
the State, the Commerce, the Treasury, and
other Departments take the attitude that their
task is to give information to the public about
their activities, while the War and Navy Depart-

ments regard it as patriotic duty to "sell" the
army and the navy to the American people.
Consider for a moment how they do this:

There are exactly 340 individual newspapers
and Press associations listed in the last Congressional Directory as members of the Senate and
House Press galleries—which means that these
maintain telegraphic correspondents in Washington. Other writers not listed in the Congressional
Directory send news and feature material by
mail. The Associated Press keeps a staff of forty
correspondents and serves about 1200 newspapers. The United Press has a staff of twenty
persons, the Universal Service and the International News Service each have twelve people.
Of individual newspapers, outside of those published in Washington itself, the *New York Times*
maintains the largest staff, being served by eleven
of its own correspondents in the national capital.

Foreign telegraphic agencies and newspapers
represented in Washington by their own correspondents are: the London *Times* and the *Morning Post*; the Wolff Bureau, the *Berliner Tage-
blatt* and the *Cologne Gazette* of Germany; the
Havas Agency and the *Petit Parisien* of France;
the Stefani Agency of Italy, recently installed; the
Telegraph Agency of the Soviet Union, briefly
called the Tass, represented by an American;
La Nacion of Buenos Aires; and *La Nacion* of
Santiago, Chile.

Foreign correspondents are given the same
facilities in Washington as American correspondents. Unlike European Governments, which
maintain foreign Press Sections in their Ministries
of Foreign Affairs to deal with foreign corre-

spondents, Washington admits them wherever American correspondents are admitted. The comparatively small showing of foreign correspondents in Washington is due to the fact that most foreign papers which maintain direct representation in the United States choose New York as their centre.

How do all these correspondents gather their news and views for the Press? In many ways Washington makes it easier, and offers greater facilities than any foreign capital. The President of the United States receives the correspondents in person regularly twice a week. They may present written questions, which he answers or not, as he sees fit. Oftentimes the information he gives is not for publication, but merely intended to serve as "background" in steering correspondents correctly as to the Government's views. The Secretary of State receives correspondents at eleven o'clock for about a quarter of an hour every morning except Tuesday. Other Cabinet officers are available at stated times.

It is the testimony of newspaper correspondents of whom inquiry was made that the War and Navy Departments are much more aggressive in "getting news across" than any of the other Government Departments. Their testimony might be summed up as follows:

"The War and Navy Departments, their officials, and the officers are 'out to sell' the army and the navy and the air force to the American people. We get more 'hand-outs' from those two departments, and they make it a point to dig out feature material for us. They want to create sentiment which will justify the large appro-

priations demanded. They send us résumés of
annual and other reports made by high officers
of the army and navy, and generals and admirals
are always ready to talk. Besides, the army and
the navy have plenty of material for photographs,
the news reels, and the moving pictures generally.
They do not hesitate to get this material to us,
and the public seems to want it."

The army and navy have certain tremendous
advantages over other departments when it comes
to providing material for the Press and interesting the Press in their activities. Newspaper correspondents can be taken on interesting expeditions
on battleships, airplanes, submarines, zeppelins
— and when newspaper men are not attached to
an expedition, officers may be assigned, one to
each news service to keep them posted as to what
happens. Reserve officers are urged "to cultivate
the Press, to furnish news items of a personal and
local nature, built around the name and address
of members of the regiment, to prepare an editorial occasionally, and to explain the principles
of national defence".

In a speech before the House of Representatives,
Representative Ross A. Collins, of Mississippi,
ranking Democratic member of the Committee on
Appropriations for the War Department, made
this statement in regard to the propaganda of
the War Department—its power to make news,
and to get its point of view before the people:

I have tried to find out the total number of army
posts, army offices, area headquarters, city-school systems, colleges, camps, and so forth, where military
officers are on duty, and having opportunities to reach the
public through speeches, personal contacts, and so forth.

I find, for example, that the Regular Army has at least 340 posts, arsenals, fields, offices, and so forth, outside Washington, and 38 procurement planning offices. The National Guard has 3203 camps, units, and offices. Military training receives Federal aid in 418 colleges and preparatory schools, and these boys go to 44 camps under 9 corps area offices. The citizens' military training camps have 89 procurement offices and camps. The National Board of Promotion of Rifle Practice has 1600 clubs. The Organised Reserves have 88 offices in 87 cities. There are many duplications in this list, but the total of 5829 is very suggestive of just how much propaganda power might be used.

Then, you must remember that these official activities have their unofficial associations backing them up in all their undertakings. The citizens' military training camps have the Citizens' Military Training Camps Association with 3400 active workers over the country. The organised Reserves have the Reserve Officers' Association with local chapters in all leading centres. The National Rifle Association backs up the National Board. And now a Reserve Officers' Training Corps Association has been formed to promote the Reserve Officers' Training Corps in schools and colleges. The poor old public will be bombarded with heavy propaganda artillery, and this Congress will be helpless unless we stop this growth now. . . .

That the Press is at least occasionally misled and deceived by agents reflecting the military point of view was made perfectly plain in the Shearer incident. It is possible that the Government itself could find means, as it did in the Shearer case, to set a limit to the amount of propaganda carried on through the War and Navy Departments, but the public must accept from the Press itself protection against the efforts of civilians and civilian associations selfishly interested in perpetuating and increasing the military machine.

The real question, however, is how can news of a military nature, inevitable and legitimate so long as the war machine exists, be offset by news which will tend to create the newer picture of a world organised on a peace basis. So far as the State Department—the branch of the Government most concerned with maintaining peace—is concerned, its contact with the Press is through a Division of Current Information. This Division, in so far as the Department's policies permit, answers inquiries from the Press. The head of the Division is always accessible to newspaper men in person or by telephone. He replies to their inquiries on his own responsibility, or gets the information they desire from the proper official, or reports that "there is nothing to say". But it is only on rare occasions that the State Department attempts to make news of its own activities. It did, for instance, in the case of the signing of the Kellogg Pact, and to a certain extent in connection with the London Naval Conference. However, most of the news that comes from the State Department is dug out by correspondents, who, in one way or another, get a tip that there is a story for the digging.

For instance, when it came time for a copy of the Preparatory Disarmament Commission's Draft Convention to arrive in Washington, a correspondent who "covers" the State Department for one of the Press Associations dug it out by going to the Western European Division, where one room is now frankly known as the "League of Nations Office". The chief of this Washington bureau agreed, and the young man wrote three brief articles, which were carried over the wires. These were the first, and for some time the only mention of that Draft Convention, which is destined to play such an important part in success or failure to demobilise the war machine. This in spite of the fact that Ambassador Gibson, the American delegate at the Preparatory Disarmament Commission, made a strong plea at the closing session at Geneva, urging Governments to educate public opinion in preparation for the world conference. No move has been made by the State Department toward that object, at least up to the time of writing this paper.

In Europe there is much closer control over the Press than in the United States. In several European countries news agencies are actually Government-owned or controlled, and a definite censorship of the Press exists. Such manipulation of the Press for political purposes, as this control makes possible, is, from every point of view, a grave danger. There seems, however, every reason why a definite effort should be made by the central Government to see that no one branch or department of the Government advertises its activities through the press in such a way that it makes it more difficult for other departments to achieve their purposes.

Since the War there has been a lamentable reluctance to assert the civilian point of view in opposition to the military; but for the civilian officers of the Government, or the citizens themselves, to fail to exercise control over the military branches is definitely to shirk responsibilities put upon them by the Constitution. One of the very interesting results of the London Naval Conference was the public statement made by the Secretary of State warning the people against being misled in their judgments by the inevitable prejudices of the military point of view constantly given widespread expression.

To summarise these various considerations in regard to the influence of the Press on problems of war and peace, it is to be noted first of all that, unless it is to be subjected to the absolute control of a central authority, it is as misleading to speak of "the Press" as it is to talk about "woman". There are many papers inevitably representing a variety of points of view, and, therefore, emphasising not only in their editorials but in their news columns various phases of world life. Accepting the Press as it is, however, there are certain factors which tend to make it an aid in establishing better international relations, and which should, therefore, be developed; and there are certain others needing to be discouraged, since their tendency is to throw the influence of the Press on the side of the maintenance of the old war system.

So far as the editorial columns and the signed articles of special correspondents are concerned, any plan such as travelling scholarships or exchange of journalists, which provides an opportunity for increased first-hand knowledge of other countries, must be of special value. Conferences of journalists themselves, consideration of the power and importance of the Press at such a conference as was recently held by the Department of Journalism at Princeton University, are also strong influences in the right direction. More study might well be given to the problems of the Press in colleges, and it would seem possible that colleges might co-operate with journalists in arranging summer conferences. Public recognition of the influence and power of members of the newspaper profession, their more frequent inclusion at least as advisers and consultants in public undertakings in any community, will also tend to call into the profession men prepared for leadership. A definite effort should be made to see that editors and special correspondents have full information as to what is being done for the promotion of better international understanding and the development of the institutions of peace, and of the conditions which necessitate peace and have given rise to these activities.

In regard to the three aspects of the news which are of special importance in international relations, in the first place, the inevitable tendency, because of the newspaper need to appeal to large numbers of people, to run sensational news can be offset in various ways. One is through unremitting protests against all unfair or misleading reports of life in other countries. An international committee, such as the journalists themselves are attempting to set up, might well be devoted to this purpose. There might also be a definite effort to interest correspondents sent into a country by foreign papers in the constructive life of the nation. They should be afforded something the same recognition as is given to the representatives of their Governments, for their power is often as great or greater.

In the second place, if the international aspects of national policies are to be brought out in the news, they must be deliberately set forth in statements by people of sufficient prominence to

give what they say a place in the news, in resolutions adopted at meetings, and through consultation with editors and two kinds of letters to
papers: (1) those written to the editor himself
asking his opinion and setting forth facts for his
consideration, and (2) those designed for publication.

In the third place, if what may be called peace
news is to compete successfully for newspaper
space with military news, a persistent effort must
be made to express the demand for peace, to call
attention to conditions which are necessitating
peace and to the activities of peace organisations
in picturesque, dramatic, "newsy" ways, which
will lead naturally to their reflection in the news
columns of the press. The old order which represents the opposition has the unusual advantage
of possessing spokesmen who are government
officials. To compete with this advantage the
peace forces must do what William James long
ago urged, they must "elect peace men to power"
so that peace arguments, ideals and purposes may
be set forth with the reality that is given to words
when there is power behind them.

But no matter how much effort is made to
make the press an influence on the side of peace,
it can never be wholly this until the change from
the old order to the new is completed. The thing
which is of first importance, therefore, is to learn
to read papers intelligently. Training in how to
read the newspapers, what difficulties in their
compilation must be allowed for, by what
internal evidence prejudice in their columns
can be detected, how daily news can be supplemented with the longer discussions to be found

M

in magazines or in what amounts to a new type
of book, "the news book", dealing with current
affairs, should be given not only in colleges but
in high schools and in so far as possible in elementary schools, for it is the foundation of intelligent citizenship. The newspaper has its own
task and function. There is no justification in
making it as it were the scapegoat for virtues
which it is the responsibility of the rest of the
community to cultivate.

VIII

THE POLITICAL CAUSES OF WAR

By Wickham Steed

War is an effort to impose the will of one country upon another by force. The political causes of war are the desires, ideals, appetites, interests, resentments or beliefs which peoples or their Governments are willing, in the last resort, to fight for. These causes would cease to produce war if a majority, or an active and directing minority, in the principal nations of the world thought it wrong or foolish to fight for them in any circumstances. A conviction that the methods of peace are adequate to deal with international disputes would, if it were widely shared and firmly held, tend to eradicate war; though, failing unanimity on this point, the same result might be attained were the nations which discountenance war prepared in all circumstances to uphold the principle that international differences shall not be settled by the victorious might of any of the parties directly involved.

Most great wars have revealed a common feature—all belligerents have believed war to be a lawful means of seeking to impose their will upon others or of resisting such imposition. The rightfulness of war as the *ultima ratio* of kings and peoples was not questioned. Hence the development of what are called "the laws of war". There would have been no sense in devising laws to regulate an unlawful undertaking. There are, for instance, no laws of piracy.

Nevertheless views of war, even as a legitimate enterprise, have undergone many changes. Monarchs and statesmen came to feel that, at least, a tolerable pretext must be found for military adventure, that it could no longer be undertaken for nakedly predatory reasons. The importance of securing popular sanction, if not of arousing popular enthusiasm for it, was increasingly appreciated. Efforts were made to endow it with a moral purpose. To this end propaganda was undertaken, never more widely and persistently than before and during the World War itself.

Upon the precise causes of and responsibility for the World War of 1914 to 1918, students of its antecedents and of its history are still far from being agreed. The thousands of official documents hitherto published leave room for many differences of opinion. Yet, long before the War broke out, contemporary observers foresaw and foretold that it would come, and how. The play of political forces in and beyond Europe was so obvious that, from the spring of 1909 onwards, the course those forces would take, in the probable event of a conflict between Austria-Hungary and Serbia, was plain to any experienced eye. Only when passions and resentments have died down, and the facts, material and psychological, have been impartially ascertained and admitted, will it be possible finally to assess degrees of "war guilt".

Meanwhile, some of the contributory causes of the World War continue to operate. The German people, for example, were persuaded that their country was threatened by a stealthy policy of "encirclement" on the part of England; and that though Austria-Hungary took the offensive against Serbia, and Germany against Belgium and France, this action was justified by the necessity of breaking through a ring of foes. The leading German authority on this subject, Professor Hermann Kantorowicz, now repudiates these beliefs as unfounded. In a monumental work *The Spirit of British Policy and the Myth of the Encirclement of Germany*, he shows, on the strength of German official documents, that the "encirclement" theory was deliberately invented in Germany. Not only, he writes, was there no hostile English policy of encirclement, but the theory of such a policy was originally put forward by German leaders "in full consciousness of its untruth, in order to create the right atmosphere for our fatal policy of naval expansion, even if it is repeated in good faith to-day. . . . When at last the truth became known to me I wrote this book with a sick heart, full of shame and indignation, and I lay it now before my countrymen, without fear and—without hope."

No fair-minded student of international affairs can deny that before 1914 and throughout the War the German people honestly believed in this myth, or that a large majority of them honestly believe it still. "To-day", adds Professor Kantorowicz, "the spectre of Encirclement has grown into a terrible reality; to-day an ill-equipped Germany sees herself surrounded by powerful antagonists who continue to fear us and whom, for this very reason, we must fear. For in this age of government by the people and of warfare by the people the decisive and almost the only cause of war is the fear of war. Who is to protect us from it?"

Undeniably, fear stands foremost among the conceivable causes of future war. It enters as largely into the outlook of Germany and of Soviet Russia as into that of Poland and France. Its removal is one of the major postulates of peace. In its present intensity and peculiar quality it is a new factor. Formerly, the inculcation of fear was, indeed, a constant aim of monarchs and States. The threat of war was ever present in international intercourse. It lay behind an ostensibly peaceful diplomacy. It gave point to the fallacious adage, "Wouldst thou have peace, prepare for war", because it was assumed that any State strong enough to make war with a good chance of success would be likely to do so. But to-day international fears are of a less positive kind. While no Government in Europe, perhaps no Government in the world, desires war, many apprehend that, somehow, war will break out. There may be little question of any direct attack by a powerful military State upon another, but there is a widespread feeling that the territorial and political changes wrought by the World War and sanctioned by the Peace Treaties—changes which were held to provide some measure of security against the recurrence of war—are so strongly resented by the peoples at whose expense they were made that war may ensue.

For these reasons the newer and truer adage,

"Wouldst thou have peace, prepare for peace"—
which was inscribed on the gold pen presented to
Mr. Kellogg by the City of Havre in readiness for
the signing of the Pact of Paris in Renunciation
of War on August 27, 1928—still finds hesitating
acceptance as a principle of national and international statecraft. Though the "will to war" no
longer exists in the same degree as it existed
before 1914; though the Pact of Paris has "outlawed war" by international compact engrossed
on solemn parchment, the purposeful organisation
of peace in security still proceeds with halting
step. Fear, lack of security, belief in the likelihood
of war lurk in an anxious background while
statesmen at Geneva and elsewhere painfully
consider how armaments can be reduced and
feelings of security be engendered. The truth
seems to be that even the international engagements directed against the recurrence of war have
outrun the normal convictions of the peoples in
whose names those engagements were entered
into.

A deeper truth is that the advocates of peace
have not yet realised how formidable is the task
which the framers of the League Covenant and of
the Pact of Paris undertook when they resolved
to impede and to ostracise war. Maybe they have
still to understand the essential nature of the
work to which they set their hands. They are still
prone to conceive peace negatively, as the mere
prevention of war, not positively as the creation
of a loftier and more dynamic type of civilisation.
The current conception of peace is still that of an
interval between inevitable wars, not that of a
new and lasting state of human society. It is too

often forgotten that, despite its destructiveness of life and wealth, war is a positive form of activity of which the appeal to men's minds and hearts has not been wholly ignoble. The most ardent partisan of peace cannot deny that war has sometimes removed abuses, broken chains, and advanced human progress. It has been a force, an expression of power, a school of discipline, of heroism, of self-devotion, an outlet for ambition, a synthesis of ideals and appetites, a supreme risk and a call to action. For countless ages it has been the chief preoccupation of mankind. Readiness and fitness to fight and to die for tribe, nation, or country have determined the scale of social honour and the very structure of society. War has been the shuttle that has woven a scarlet thread into the grey tissue of human existence. It has often aroused, sometimes in combination, two of the most potent instincts in human nature—the instinct of self-preservation and the instinct of self-sacrifice. A third and by no means negligible element in it has been the willingness, nay, the desire of many men to obey authorised commands, to cease to think and to feel as detached individuals, to live, to march, and to fight in disciplined masses, to take no thought for the morrow and to care only for the doing of each day's duty under orders unquestioned and unquestionable. All these instincts have their place in the causes of war; and from them the conclusion seems to flow that not until they can be harnessed to the enterprise of peace as firmly as they have been linked with the waging of war, will peace rest upon firm psychological foundations.

Is it not presumptuous to imagine that it will
be enough to say: "No more war!" without offer-
ing mankind a vigorous substitute for it, in order
to change the object of deep-rooted habits of
feeling and thought? To-day the real case against
war is its unworthiness as an occupation for
civilised beings, a *reductio ad absurdum* of human
intelligence. Yet its unworthiness will not abolish
it unless peace be worthier. Peace cannot triumph
until it offers openings for fuller heroism, for the acceptance of higher risks, for readier self-sacrifice
than those which mechanised, chemicalised, scientific warfare can now hold out. Many thinkers
on war and peace have fallen into the error of
conceiving peace, as it were, "in the flat", of
looking upon it as a kind of static negative, as
opposed to war which is a dynamic positive.
They have appealed to the reasonable minds of
calm human beings, and have put forward ex-
cellent arguments why men and nations should
not engage in a venture of uncertain profit and
certain loss, such as war, and why they should
devote all their energies to the profitable pursuits
of peace. One well-known plea, often to be heard
before the World War, was that war could not
occur because it would not pay. The financial and
economic truth of this plea did not save it from
the gross error of assuming that the behaviour
of men, either as individuals or in the mass, is always determined by nice calculations of material
profit and loss. Under normal conditions it may,
to some extent, be thus determined; and, within
limits, it is true that the economic forces to which
Karl Marx, in his materialist interpretation
of history, assigned pre-eminence as factors in

human progress, are decisive motives of human action. But in moments of crisis—and most wars arise in or through moments of crisis—it is not true that cool calculations of interest override uncalculating passion. The emotional side of human nature is stronger than the intellectual, and when men's passions are sufficiently wrought upon, they are capable of the most uneconomic decisions and deeds. Afterwards they may ruefully reckon profit and loss, and resolve to be guided by reason in future. Yet a fresh emergency is likely to find them, or their offspring, not less ready to throw calm reflection to the winds and to give rein to emotions which reason may be powerless to control.

Now passion will not be quenched while humanity lasts. The problem of removing the causes of war is, in large measure, the problem of finding ways of enlisting men's passions not only against war itself, but in the service of a new ideal of constructive human civilisation from which war "as an instrument of national policy" shall have been banned as foolish, barbaric, and unworthy. When the thought of war has become as repugnant to individuals in the majority of civilised nations as the thought of murder for personal gain is to-day, there will be a prospect of establishing the methods of peace as the only tolerable form of international activity.

The chief impediment to progress in this direction has hitherto lain in the unreadiness of nations to abate their national sovereignties. The process of peace is analogous to that by which restrictions of personal sovereignty were imposed upon individuals in organised communities. This process

was slow. Long after the equality of citizens before the law had been proclaimed in principle and
recognised in practice, it was tacitly admitted,
even in highly civilised countries, that individuals
were entitled to defend their personal honour or
that of their families in armed combat. The
practice of duelling long persisted, nay, still per-
sists in countries like Germany, France, and
Italy, and it was only suppressed in England a
century ago. To insist that all citizens must be
subservient to the law, even in matters of honour,
was long felt to be an intolerable interference
with personal freedom. Similarly, the right of
nations to engage in duelling, that is to say, war,
has been stubbornly defended despite the growing sense that nations are increasingly inter-
dependent and are coming to form, to all intents
and purposes, a real international community.
If it be argued that all international treaties imply limitations of national sovereignty, and that
a general treaty outlawing war, such as the Pact
of Paris, is merely an extension of this principle,
it must be remembered that there is a distinction
between such treaties, unaccompanied by definite
"sanctions", and the limitations of sovereignty
involved in the enforcement of the outlawry of war
upon lawless members of an international community by the concerted action or the superior
authority of its law-abiding members.

For a long time it was customary to exclude
from the scope of international arbitration those
disputes which might be held to affect the honour
or the vital interests of the parties to arbitration
treaties. Though this restriction has disappeared
from recent treaties, notably from those com-

prised in the Locarno Settlement of October 1925, and from the Pact of Paris in renunciation of war, nations are still reluctant to refer matters affecting their honour or vital interests to the decision of an international tribunal or to that of third parties who would certainly be foreign. The truth is that international compacts restricting the supreme affirmation of a nation's sovereignty—its right to make war—are in advance of public opinion and of public feeling in the several nations whose Governments have entered into such compacts.

Thus we return to the point that a potent cause of war, and a principal impediment to the creation of assured peace, resides in the state of public opinion or public feeling upon the lawfulness of war. Opinion and feeling, in their turn, depend upon the knowledge which a people possesses of controverted matters affecting it. Were it possible to spread information of unquestioned accuracy upon all questions that bear upon international relations, and to secure for such information unhesitating acceptance by all whom it may concern, the risk that emotional explosions may be brought about by propaganda or, to give it its true name, by partial and deliberately misleading statements, would be greatly diminished. Much of the danger of war to-day arises from the incompatible views of ascertainable facts that are entertained in various countries. With good reason one of the shrewdest students of international affairs has affirmed his belief that, in the last resort, the potential causes of war can only be removed by definite arrangements for "fact-finding in concert".

The existence of these causes is undeniable. Some of them are directly related to the course and outcome of the World War and to the Peace Treaties which followed it. The most powerful of them is the persistence, not to say the fostering, of a sense of injustice among some peoples, and the denial by others that injustice has been done. In several regions of Europe it is claimed, for instance, that the retention under alien rule of large minorities of people who belong ethnically to other States is inimical to any lasting peace. The counter-claim, that frontiers ethnically perfect are politically and geographically impracticable, possesses no little force, nor can it be doubted that the present order in Europe is less imperfect than was the pre-war order which held in subjection to alien rulers far larger minorities than those whose lot is now alleged to be intolerable. Moreover, in post-war Europe there exist, under the League of Nations, sundry means of inquiring into and of mitigating acknowledged hardships. But when this delicate and complicated subject is closely examined, the pregnant conclusion emerges that the position of minorities, and many other disputed issues, would be susceptible of friendly settlement did not the maintenance of present political divisions appear to those who uphold them a valuable element of national security in case of war.

Ever since the conclusion of the Peace Treaties, and despite the embodiment in them of the Covenant of the League of Nations, this question of "security" has lain at the root of international anxieties. By dint of discussion, "security" has come to mean the political and territorial safety of France, and of the nations allied with her, against attack from outside. No analysis of the political causes of war can avoid a frank examination of this issue; and it will be well briefly to trace its history.

In its present form, the question of French security is a result of the invasion of Belgium and France by German armies in August 1914, and of the continued occupation of the invaded regions by German forces for more than four years. Even after the adoption of the League Covenant by the Paris Peace Conference on February 14, 1919, and despite the assumption that the United States would belong to the League, the military advisers of the French Government could only be prevented from insisting that French security required the annexation, or the permanent occupation, of German territory on the left bank of the Rhine, by an Anglo-American promise to help France in case she should be exposed to German attack. The rejection of the Peace Treaties in the United States deprived this guarantee of much of its value, and its remaining value was destroyed when Great Britain declined to uphold individually an undertaking which her Prime Minister had given jointly with the President of the United States. Similarly, the worth of the "sanctions" against war that are provided in the League Covenant were enfeebled by the withdrawal of the United States and by the effects of that withdrawal upon Great Britain. President Wilson's view that "in the League there will be no neutrals", and that Covenant-breaking States would have no belligerent rights, was not only upset by the American repudiation

of the League, but Great Britain was obliged to
reflect upon her own position should she, on behalf of the League, take action likely to antagon-
ise a United States which had become neutral
and potentially hostile toward the League itself.
Therefore, and apart from the fact that the
League Covenant left open four distinct contingencies in which members of the League might
lawfully wage war—contingencies in which non-
belligerent members of the League would be
entitled to claim neutral rights—the French
people felt that the League of Nations had become inadequate to safeguard their security.

Mainly for this reason efforts were made at
Geneva in 1923 and 1924 to supplement the
League Covenant by pacts providing for mutual
assistance between the parties to them against
any aggressor, the aggressor being defined as the
State or States which should resort to war in
defiance of international obligations to settle disputes by peaceful means. The results of these
efforts were the Draft Treaty of Mutual Assistance of 1923, and the Geneva Protocol for the
Pacific Settlement of International Disputes in
1924. Both of these instruments were, however,
destroyed by the decision of successive British
Governments—the Labour Government of 1924
and the Conservative Government of 1924 to 1929.
Though many reasons were assigned for these
British decisions, the true reason was never
officially admitted. It was that Great Britain
desired not to be drawn into a conflict with
the United States, as she might be if she bound
herself absolutely to take action in support of
the League Covenant on the lines of the Draft

Treaty or of the Geneva Protocol. The one exception to this aspect of British policy was furnished by the main Locarno Treaty, or Western Security Pact, of 1925, by which Great Britain and Italy undertook to come to the help of France and Belgium or Germany, in case any of them should be attacked in the Rhineland region. Thus Great Britain (though not the British Commonwealth of Nations as a whole) guaranteed the security of the Eastern frontiers of France and Belgium and of the Western frontiers of Germany. It was, however, an essential condition of this guarantee that Germany should enter the League of Nations.

But, on admission to the League, Germany speedily raised the important issue of equality in armaments. Dr. Stresemann gave notice that his country would not and could not tolerate indefinitely a position in which Germany was compulsorily disarmed while the armaments of her neighbours remained at a high level. He appealed to the Preamble of the military, naval and air clauses of the Peace Treaties, which stated that the disarmament of Germany would "facilitate the initiation" of disarmament in other countries. He appealed further to Article VIII of the League Covenant of which the first part of the first paragraph recognises that "the maintenance of peace requires the reduction of national armaments to the lowest point consistent with national safety" —or, as the French text puts it, "national security". Dr. Stresemann did not lay equal or, indeed, any emphasis upon the second part of the first paragraph of Article VIII which cites "the enforcement of international obligations by com-

mon action" as a twin factor in determining the
level to which armaments should be reduced.
Yet it is precisely on this twin factor that the
French thesis of "security" insists.

Although the Geneva Protocol was rejected
by Great Britain, two significant consequences
flowed from it. It inspired the German suggestion
for a Western Security Pact that led, in October
1925, to the Locarno Settlement. It proposed,
besides, the holding of a General Disarmament
Conference in 1925, upon the success of which
the validity of the Protocol itself was to depend.
The British rejection of the Protocol, which had
provided for security by mutual assistance, inevitably postponed the General Disarmament
Conference, and left the problem of security unsolved. For this reason, also, the work of the
League's Preparatory Disarmament Commission,
which was set up at the end of 1925, proceeded
slowly; and it was not until December 1930 that
substantial agreement could be reached upon a
Draft Disarmament Convention as a basis for the
General Disarmament Conference at Geneva in
1932.

Meanwhile, several attempts had been made,
apart from the League, to limit and to reduce
naval armaments. Of these attempts the chief
were the Washington and London Naval Conferences of 1921–22 and 1930, both of which
yielded valuable results; and the Three-Power
Naval Conference, between the United States,
Great Britain, and Japan at Geneva in 1927,
which ended in total failure. Before the London
Naval Conference of 1930 the French Government frankly declared that any serious reduction

N

of naval armaments must depend upon the provision of security by mutual assistance. The Conference avoided this issue and dealt solely with the technique of naval limitation. It could not be induced even to define the function of naval armaments, reduced or unreduced, in a world which, by the Paris Peace Pact of 1928, had renounced war.

The feeling of insecurity, and the fears which it engenders, are undoubtedly the strongest potential causes of war in the world to-day. No nation, whether it belong to the League or not, and no signatory of the Paris Peace Pact, can be certain that, if it reduces its armaments to a point at which it would have to rely upon the help of others for defence against attack, such help would really be forthcoming. It cannot even be sure that the attacking nation would be effectively outlawed and opposed by the rest of the world. Hence, argue those nations which feel insecure, the difficulty of reaching such a degree of international disarmament as is indispensable to the organisation of peace. Against the thesis— mainly French, though undeniably in harmony with the original purpose and spirit of the League Covenant—which makes disarmament depend upon the provision of effective security, other theses are stoutly upheld. They are that the danger of war cannot be removed by a preponderance of armed strength even against eventual war-makers; that the right path to security lies through disarmament, not *vice versa*, since the existence of strong armaments inspires fear, and tends, in the long run, to produce counter-armaments and war; and that the only certain means of attaining security would be for all the nations which have renounced war to prove their sincerity by restricting the wherewithal for the waging of war.

A supplementary argument against the "security" thesis is that, inasmuch as the order of things established by the Peace Treaties is vitiated by manifest injustices, it cannot be healthy or permanent unless those injustices are redressed; and that peace-loving nations ought not to promise to support it by force lest injustice be perpetuated, and, with it, the danger of justified revolt and war.

To this argument an apparently cogent answer is returned. It is that the provision of security against war is not, and cannot be, a guarantee of any *status quo*; that the essence of security is a valid undertaking to ban war even as a means of redressing real or alleged wrong; and that, once this security has been provided, inquiry into and the redress of wrongs could be fearlessly made in a warless world.

International discussion upon security, disarmament, and the prevention of war now stands at the point marked by these theses and arguments. This discussion dominated the field of international peace thought on the eve of the General Disarmament Conference. Unless some practical synthesis between opposing views can be found, the success of the Disarmament Conference may be imperilled. Should the Conference fail, the danger of war would be likely to increase, because the sense of insecurity would be accentuated by despair of finding adequate means to remove the causes of war. Influential representatives of

Germany have, for instance, already advocated the withdrawal of their country from the League, and the repudiation of the Disarmament clauses of the Peace Treaties, in case the Disarmament Conference should not succeed in reducing international armaments practically to the level which the Peace Treaty imposed upon Germany. German withdrawal from the League would undoubtedly invalidate the Locarno Settlement and throw Europe back into the perplexities of the early post-war years. So strong is the belief of the German people in the "war innocence" of their country, and so unanimous their resentment of the alleged injustice of the Peace Settlement, that they are not far from holding themselves morally entitled and, indeed, bound by every dictate of national self-respect, to break by force the chains that bind them, and, if all else fails, to vindicate their good right on the battlefield.

France and her associates, well aware of this state of feeling in Germany, believe, on the other hand, that the object of German policy is not so much to reduce armaments as to gain for Germany freedom to re-arm. They allege that, despite the compulsory reduction of German regular forces to 100,000 men, and the destruction of immense quantities of German war material, Germany has adopted a system of secret armaments and of clandestine military training which would enable her to put into the field a formidable army at very short notice. Besides, the German military authorities are known to have cultivated an understanding with the Russian Red Army, and are suspected of having framed, with the Soviet military authorities, joint stra-

tegic plans for eventual operations against Poland, the ally of France. In these circumstances,
and pending proof that German intentions are
really pacific, France and her allies are reluctant
to reduce their armaments to the level which the
stipulations of the League Covenant and the
Preamble to the Disarmament clauses of the
Versailles Treaty clearly foreshadow.

These differences of outlook, and the fears
which inspire them, are among the chief causes
of possible war in Europe. Behind them lies,
however, a more subtle difference upon which
neither the French nor the Germans are wont to
insist. It is, nevertheless, real. It consists in the
view, widely entertained in France and in other
Western European countries but repudiated in
Germany, that, after their victory in 1918, the
United States and its European associates earnestly sought to establish Western civilisation
upon a new basis, and to eliminate war, both as
an instrument of national policy and as a means
of settling international disputes. To this end
they agreed to the embodiment of the League
Covenant in the Peace Treaties, to the provision
of some degree of protection for ethnical minorities, and to the principle of the reduction of
armaments to the lowest level consistent with
national security and with the enforcement of
international obligations under the auspices of
the League. These facts are held to substantiate
the claim that the authors of the Peace Treaties
were not devoid of honest idealism, and that they
took what may be called a regenerate view of
future international relationships. If Germany,
it is argued, would recognise the sincerity of this

idealism, if her people could, in their turn, adopt a regenerate view of the future instead of clinging to pre-war methods and conceptions, they would place themselves on a footing of moral equality with other enlightened nations, and would facilitate the attainment of political and military equality.

As long as these fundamental differences last it will not be easy to eradicate belief in the likelihood of war—which is the true source of insecurity— and to replace it by a conviction that, since war is so unlikely as to be a negligible contingency, the only sane course for civilised peoples is to seek mutual understanding and to join in mitigating or obliterating acknowledged hardships or wrongs. The thought that war itself may, after all, still be the supreme arbiter between nations is assuredly the main obstacle to the creation of peace. This truth was obviously in the mind of M. Briand, when, at the close of his address to the League Assembly on September 11, 1931, he said that, in order to ensure the success of the Disarmament Conference, it would suffice for the nations attending it "solemnly to declare, and realising all the implications which those words entail, 'No more war!' We do not admit, in any event, for any reason, in any circumstance, that war which we have nailed to the pillory as a crime shall again raise its head unpunished."

The implications to which M. Briand referred were emphasised by the delegate of Spain, Don Salvador de Madariaga, whose authority on the subject of disarmament is unchallenged. He urged that not even the reduction of the numeri-

cal totals of arms and of military or naval bud-
gets can furnish a guarantee of warlessness. It is
too often forgotten, he continued, that the per-
fecting of military technique and organisation
allows all States actually to increase their power
of eventual aggression, while decreasing their
ostensible armaments and the outlay upon them.
A whole psychology of precaution, defence, and
distrust induces Governments actively to pursue
research in preparation for chemical warfare,
after having prohibited the use of poison gas. It
would be useful, he claimed, to return to the
spirit of the League Covenant—a spirit frankly
hostile to war—and to establish, by a one-clause
agreement among members of the League, that
the Covenant means what it says, and that they
are prepared to carry it out. Taken together, the
Covenant of the League and the Pact of Paris
in renunciation of war form a powerful combination. This combination compels members of the
League to admit that, for them at any rate, neutrality is dead. But, as Don Salvador de Madariaga insisted, a serious difficulty arises in regard
to States that are not members of the League;
and, in his words, it is a duty of fundamental
sincerity for members of the League, respectfully
and frankly, to say to such States that, while the
reasons which oblige them to stay outside the
League are recognised, "it is an unquestionable
fact that, so long as the United States of America
and the Union of Soviet Republics have not
joined with us in a system that shall forever
banish neutrality, the ideal of integral disarmament can never be attained".

These public declarations by the representa-

tives of France and of Spain indicate the major
term of the problem of eliminating the political
causes of war. Another of its terms is suggested
by the question: "What is the lawful function of
armaments in a world that has renounced war?"
To this question there is only one comprehensive
answer. Since war as an instrument of national
policy has been renounced, and, by renunciation,
ostracised; since armaments cannot lawfully be
used save in self-defence or in collective action
against a law-breaker, their lawful function is
no other than a police function, individually or
jointly discharged, in the service of an international law which the outlawry of war has
revolutionised.

The struggle for peace and for the elimination
of the causes of war is a struggle for the enthrone-
ment of law over lawless force. The function of
lawful force is to be a terror to evil-doers and to
comfort the law-abiding, who, deeming themselves secure under the aegis of a law strongly
supported by lawful force, may relinquish their
own aggressive power and accept impartial ad-
judication upon their international claims. The
postulate of international, as of social, peace is
that the law should be, and should be known to
be, strong and strongly supported by public
feeling. When this postulate has been fulfilled,
the political causes of war will disappear, and the
path of mankind will run toward the highest and
hardest task men have ever essayed--the creation
of peace.

SUPPLEMENTARY

I

NATIONAL MONOPOLIES OF RAW MATERIALS

By Jacob Viner

THERE are at least three types of international problems arising out of monopolies of raw materials. First, there is the problem of securing equal access, as between national and foreign capital and enterprise, or as between the capital and enterprise of different foreign countries, to the opportunity of exploiting undeveloped natural resources such as minerals, forests, or fisheries. Second, there is the problem of the private trust or cartel, national or international, which, without Government assistance or participation, exercises a monopoly control over some raw material. Third, there is the problem of a national (or international territorial monopoly of a raw material, which is established, and which operates with the participation and assistance, or even under the direct auspices, of the Government (or Governments) of the territory in which that monopoly exists. It is only with the last of these problems that the present memorandum attempts to deal. The first problem is a special phase of the general question of the open door with respect to trade and investments. The second problem is similarly a special phase of the general trust question. The problem of *Government* control of the export of a raw material of which the world's supply can come only or mainly from its territory is a problem more or less distinct and requiring individual treatment. It is this problem with which the present memorandum concerns itself, and only in its peacetime aspects.

The problem of territorial monopolies is essentially a problem of raw materials. Given the availability of the necessary raw materials, there will almost always be a large number of countries which can engage in the manufacture of any fabricated article, although not, of course, under equally favourable circumstances. Except for a few commodities, such as special types of wine or cheese, the final processes of whose manufacture must take place in close proximity to the place of production of their raw materials, the production of any important manufactured product is not likely to be restricted to a single region or country. Even the patent system cannot be made to support the establishment of regional monopolies, since many countries make the validity of patents subject to the condition that the patented commodity be produced within their territory. I know of no instance of an important manufactured article whose production is confined to a single country. But the production of raw materials can take place subject only to the geographical distribution of the necessary climatic and soil conditions or of mineral deposits, and where these happen to be available only in a

single region or in a few localities, the opportunity
is present for the Government (or the Governments acting in combination), within whose jurisdiction such region (or regions) is found, to exploit its monopoly position to the prejudice of the
rest of the world.

The mere fact of regional limitation of the
sources of supply of a commodity is under peacetime conditions of no special significance, except
in the obvious sense that any country which has
no rich natural resources of a particular kind is
less well off than if it had, other things remaining
the same. Regional limitation gives rise to a special
international problem only if advantage is taken
of the limitation to secure for those in the favoured
region either exclusive use of the raw material or
exorbitant prices upon its sale to foreigners. In
order that such advantage shall be obtained by a
region which is alone endowed with a particular
kind of raw material, there must be established
a restrictive or "monopolistic" control, direct or
indirect, over its export.

Most raw materials are produced by many
small-scale producers, who, because of their
number and their individualistic traditions, are
not likely to succeed in establishing, or, once established, in maintaining, a monopolistic organisation of their own accord. Even where there
are only a comparatively few large-scale producers, the lure of the extra profits which any one
independent concern can gain if all the others
combine and operate on the monopoly basis,
while it stays outside, always makes it difficult to
obtain full participation on a voluntary basis in a
monopolistic combination of all the producers in

any industry. In a small number of cases, confined
almost wholly to minerals, the private producers
of a particular raw material have been so few
that they have succeeded in organising a world-
monopoly without more assistance from their
Governments than was involved in the absence of
any explicit mark of disapproval of their activities. But, even when private initiative would
suffice to establish a monopoly, a Government
may participate in its organisation and management in order to obtain a share of its profits for
the national Treasury, to prevent its disintegration under the pressure of internal conflicts of
interest and policy, or to make certain that the
domestic consumers shall not share alike with
foreign consumers the burdens of the monopolistic exactions. In almost all cases, therefore,
of attempts to exploit the monopolistic possibilities of a regional limitation of sources of supply
of important commodities, there has either been
more or less complete failure from the start, or the
monopoly control has been established by the
Governments acting alone or in co-operation with
the producers. Whether rightly or wrongly, the
element of Government intervention in such
controls has attracted to them more attention,
and made them more serious sources of friction
in international relations than if they had been
established through private initiative alone. It is
partly the fact that monopolies of raw materials
are commonly regarded as a more serious economic menace to the material interests of other
countries than would be monopolies of manufactured commodities, partly the consideration
that a foreign monopoly is commonly regarded as

more objectionable if it is the result of Government intervention, that justifies the separate consideration of Government raw material monopolies.

Government procedure in exploiting a territorial monopoly may take any one, or any combination, of the following forms: (1) the establishment of a State-owned and controlled monopoly of production, or of export, or of both; (2) the regulation of the volume of export through fixed or sliding-scale export taxes; (3) the direct limitation of exports through outright prohibition, export quotas, or export licences; (4) the legislative or administrative limitation of production, and so indirectly of export also; and (5) Government encouragement of, and even insistence upon, the establishment by the producers themselves of a private monopoly-organisation of the industry, as a whole, or of its export activities, to be operated under private managment but in accordance with Government policy. All of these procedures are characterised by the existence of an element, varying in degree and directness, of Government intervention in the management of the industry.

When a Government establishes or promotes a control of exports in order to exploit the opportunities afforded by the existence within the limits of its jurisdiction of a more or less complete world-monopoly of some raw material, its particular objectives may be some one, or some combination, of the following: (1) to promote conservation of an exhaustible natural resource; (2) to reserve for domestic industry the conversion of the raw material into a more finished commodity; (3) to augment the State revenues at the expense of foreign consumers; (4) to "stabilise" the price of the monopolised commodity, or (5) to secure to domestic producers a higher price than they would obtain in the absence of the control of export.

Illustrative of control of export for conservation purposes are the export restrictions and high export taxes to which scarce wild animals are subject in many African countries. Conservation is stated to be also one of the purposes of the Canadian provincial restrictions on the export of pulpwood in the raw state. It should be noted, however, that where, as in the case of Canadian pulpwood, there is an important domestic market, a restriction on export which leaves domestic consumption free from control is likely to be neither highly effective as a conservation measure nor seriously intended as such. In any case, the intent of such a measure is clearly that if any conservation is to be effected thereby, its cost shall be borne by foreign consumers of the product. Export restrictions for conservation purposes have in practice been few and of minor importance.

The preservation or acquisition for the labour and capital of the raw-material producing country of the industry of conversion of the raw material to a more finished commodity was the purpose of the English prohibitions on the export of wool, hides, metals, and other crude products during the seventeenth and eighteenth centuries, and of similar export restrictions in other countries during the same period. In modern times, such has been the main purpose of the Canadian provincial restrictions on the export of pulpwood and of water-power, of the British taxes on the exports of Malay tin ore to countries outside the British Empire, of the export taxes and prohibitions in European countries on hides, rags, and bones. The purpose of such export restrictions is to withhold from foreign countries the materials in their *raw*, but not in their fabricated form, and thus to force their domestic fabrication.

The levy of export taxes on raw materials cannot of itself be taken as demonstrative of a purpose to force foreign consumers to contribute to the State revenues of the producing country, unless all or a large proportion of the world's supply of that raw material is produced in that country, other exports are left untaxed, or are taxed at much lower rates, and the rate of tax is high. In many countries producing mainly raw materials for export, and especially in tropical and sub-tropical countries, export taxes are a routine form of taxation without special significance to the outside world. In countries where the standard of living and the average holding of property is low, there is often unavailable any other form of tax which will reach effectively the great bulk of the population. Where export taxes are levied on raw materials it is necessary, therefore, to consider the severity of the tax and the accompanying circumstances before it can be determined whether or not they are being used with the purpose or the consequence of exploiting a monopoly position at the expense of foreigners. Probably the outstanding case of an export control of this type was the Chilean export tax on nitrates, which for many years produced more than half of the total revenues of the Chilean Government. With the development of competition from the artificial nitrate industry, however, it is now doubtful whether much of this export tax is borne by the foreign consumer, and it seems more probable that the greater part of it is borne by the Chilean producers.

In many cases the professed aim of export controls is the "stabilisation" of price, *i.e.* its maintenance at an approximately even and presumably "reasonable" level, free from sharp fluctuations. "Stabilisation", however, is often a euphemism for increase of price to as high a level as the traffic can be made to bear. There is no case on record in which an export control has been established with the objective of stabilising price at a level lower than, or even just equal to, that prevailing at the date of establishment of the control. This is, of course, not decisive demonstration that the objective of "stabilisation" projects is to exact unreasonably high prices from foreign consumers, since the need for export control is most likely to be felt, and the obstacles, internal and external, to its establishment most easily surmounted, when the industry is in a state of distress owing to over-development, and a resultant abnormally low price for its product. The British rubber control was established at a time when the rubber-growing industry appeared to be facing disaster, owing to the ruinously low prices which were then prevailing for rubber, and the stated aim of the control was to stabilise the price at a level higher than that then prevailing, but not clearly unreasonable in relation to the then prevailing costs of production. But when world market conditions, in conjunction with the inadequately flexible export control, forced prices up to what was indisputably an unreasonable high level, the control provisions were revised in the direction of greater rather than lesser severity. In other cases, for example, the Yucatan sisal control and the pre-war Prussian potash control, the objective was admittedly to raise the price which foreigners should pay, without reference to cost of production.[1] It may be taken for granted that most export controls aim at raising the price to foreign consumers to as high a level as is consistent with maintaining a satisfactory volume of exports. Where there is an important body of domestic consumers the control is generally devised so as to throw the burden of the higher prices wholly on the foreign consumers, and even to establish for domestic consumers prices lower than could be expected to prevail in the absence of control. Such was not the case, however, with respect to the British rubber control, which did not discriminate between British and foreign consumers of rubber.

How serious is the problem of national monopolies of raw materials, actual or prospective? A recent study of the problem lists eighteen commodities which are at present or have recently been subject to Government export con-

---

[1] Compare Delbrück, Prussian Minister of Commerce, in *Prussian Landstag*, Feb. 13, 1906: "It is my belief that the policy of the Potash Syndicate up to the present time can on the whole meet every criticism. We have succeeded in fixing prices considerably higher abroad than at home; the high prices abroad have enabled us to supply potash to domestic agriculture in general at reduced prices."

trols.[1] While it is not, and is not claimed to be, a complete list, no control of any commercial importance is omitted. Of the controls listed, several of the most important have collapsed or are at the point of collapse, *e.g.* rubber, sugar, coffee. At least one-third deal with commodities of negligible commercial importance, except to their producers, *e.g.* citrate of lime, kauri-gum, currants, pearlshell, sandalwood oil. Few of the controls deal with even approximately complete regional monopolies, and, whatever their objectives, most of them are in a position to exercise only a mild degree of influence on world prices. Of the controls whose chief objective is to raise prices to foreign consumers, probably the most important, if duration and effectiveness are taken into account, is the potash control. More important, probably, than the price controls are the controls intended to conserve for the fabricating industries of the producing country, and, in the case of colonial raw materials, of the mother country, the domestic supplies of essential raw materials, although these ordinarily attract less attention than the price controls. The most important examples of such controls are the preferential export tax on British Malayan tin, the

---

[1] Wallace and Edminster, *International Control of Raw Materials*, Institute of Economics, Washington, D.C., p. 13. The commodities and the controlling countries are as follows: camphor (Japan); citrate of lime (Italy); coffee (Brazil); cotton, long staple (Egypt); currants (Greece); kauri-gum (New Zealand); mercury (Spain, Italy); nitrate (Chile); pearlshell (Australia); potash (France, Germany); pulpwood (Canada); rubber (British Malaya—control abolished Nov. 1, 1928); sandalwood oil (British India); silk (Japan); sisal (Yucatan); sugar (Cuba—control operative 1925–28 only); sulphur (Sicily); tin (Federated Malay States).

Canadian provincial and the Newfoundland re-
trictions on the export of pulpwood, and the
restrictions on the export of electric current in
force in some of the Canadian provinces and in
some other countries.

Most of the existing and recently abolished
controls have been established since 1900—
during the period 1860 to 1900 few controls were
in existence—so there has been somewhat of
a revival in the twentieth century of the old
mercantilist policy of exploitation of regional
monopolies of raw materials. Some of the price
controls have succeeded in maintaining prices at
high levels for many years, and even some of the
controls which have collapsed succeeded in boom
years at least in raising prices to exorbitant levels.
But the experience of such price controls is, on
the whole, not such as to give great encouragement for their continual maintenance, or to indicate favourable prospects for the extension of
export control on a substantial scale to additional
commodities. While theoretically it is possible
for a country exercising control over much less
than half of the world output to exercise some
control over world price, any producing country
which attempts to control price without complete control of output must itself undergo all of
the restriction of output while the other producing countries share equally in the advantages
of the increased price. Suppose that a country
controlling 50 per cent of the world output of a
commodity wants to raise price by 20 per cent,
and that a 10 per cent reduction in world output
is necessary to secure a 20 per cent increase in
world price. It will be necessary, therefore, to

reduce output in that country by 20 per cent to
secure an increase in price of 20 per cent, provided the other producing countries do not increase their output as price rises. If, as experience
proves to be highly likely, the other countries do
increase their output when price rises, then the
country operating the control must reduce its
output still more to compensate for the increased
output of the other producers. The smaller the
proportion of the output in the country operating
the control to the total world output, and the
greater the reduction in world supply necessary
to bring about a given percentage of increase in
the world price, the greater is the proportion in
which the country operating the control must
reduce its output to obtain a given increase in
price. Under the circumstances, an export control is likely to yield substantial profits only if:
(1) it controls a good deal more than half of the
world output prior to the establishment of control; (2) there are no important potential sources
of supply requiring only a moderate increase in
price to make their exploitation profitable; (3)
there are no readily available substitutes and
consumption will not fall off sharply as price
is increased. There are few commodities which
can meet successfully all of these conditions for
any substantial period of time. The problem of
national monopolies of raw materials, in so far
at least as controls with the object of raising
world prices are concerned, is a minor problem,
and gives no occasion for serious alarm. Notori-
ously so at the present moment, and also re-
peatedly in the past, the essential problem with
respect to raw materials has been rather how

producers could find markets for their output at even barely remunerative prices rather than how consumers could obtain access to supplies at prices which were not exorbitant. With the improvement in transportation, the progressive exploration of the potential resources of even the most isolated portions of the globe, and the development of industrial and chemical technique which makes available a constantly increasing range of substitute commodities and of alternative methods of production, what menace there is in the existence or potentiality of national raw material monopolies is becoming increasingly less, rather than more, serious.

Though there is no occasion, therefore, for hysteria, there is a problem, nevertheless, in national monopoly controls. The fact that there is a general, and probably inevitable, tendency to exaggerate the extent to which such controls prevail and are effective makes the problem important, even if it exists more in imagination than in reality. International difficulties are the results of supposed conflicts of interest, and even if they arise out of illusions it is well to remove, if possible, the circumstances which give rise to these illusions. Perhaps because of their comparative rarity, export controls create proportionately more resentment and fear in foreign countries than do import controls in the form of customs tariffs of greater effectiveness and greater potentiality for injury to foreign economic interests. Power of fairly effective exploitation of consumers in a neighbouring foreign country may exist, moreover, especially for bulky commodities, even when there is no question of the possibility of exercising control over world prices. National export controls having as their objective the reservation for domestic fabrication of domestic supplies of raw materials may especially succeed in injuring neighbouring countries even though there is nothing even distantly approaching a world monopoly. The British export restrictions on tin ore appear to have been definitely responsible for the failure of a tin smelting industry to establish itself in the United States. The Canadian provincial restrictions on the export of pulpwood appear likewise to have been in large part responsible for the extensive migration which has occurred of wood pulp and paper mills from the northern United States to Canada. But the stimulus to domestic fabrication through export duties on raw materials is so closely parallel to the stimulus to domestic industry through import duties on finished products that in a world in which the latter are accepted as a normal and unobjectionable, even though regrettable, phenomenon, there would seem to be no logical justification for the common tendency to regard export duties on raw materials as a peculiarly offensive violation of international comity. Finally, the potentialities of really effective and dangerous monopoly control of raw materials become much more impressive if the possibilities of joint or simultaneous control by two or more countries, such as the Franco-German potash control and the Italo-Spanish mercury controls, are surveyed.

Given the existence of the problem, there are four possible types of procedure for coping with it: (1) unilateral, and (2) co-operative defensive or retaliatory measures by the consuming countries; (3) bilateral; and (4) multinational agreements, in which both exporting and importing countries participate, for the suppression or restriction of commodity controls.

Consuming countries which believe themselves injured by the commodity controls applied to raw materials by producing countries may either singly or in combination adopt defensive measures, such as the promotion of the development of new sources of supply, of substitutes, or of alternative methods of production, which reduce their dependence on the controlled commodities; or they may adopt retaliatory measures, such as discriminatory import duties on other commodities in which the offending countries are interested or export restrictions on such of their own raw materials as are of importance to the consumers or the industries of the offending country. A provision of this character in the United States Tariff Act of 1930 (Par. 1401) authorises the President, upon failure to secure the removal of export restrictions or export taxes on pulpwood, wood pulp, or paper, imposed by any foreign country, to impose upon uncoated printing paper an additional duty of 10 per cent *ad valorem* plus an amount equal to the export duty levied by that foreign country. Retaliatory measures of this sort, however, are generally costly to the country adopting them, and it is difficult for the Government of the country against which they are applied to abolish the offending practices without arousing domestic resentment on the ground that it has yielded unnecessarily and humiliatingly to foreign threats.

If concerted action of this sort, however, were taken by a number of important countries, it would probably prove to be a fairly effective procedure. It would probably be difficult, however, to obtain concerted action, especially as each of the injured countries would be hesitant to assume the onus of taking the initiative of organising such action. In any case, there appears to be no historical instance of concerted action of a retaliatory kind directed against export restrictions.

Under the auspices of the League of Nations, an effort has been under way to obtain by international agreement the suppression of export (and also import) controls. In accordance with a rather mild and evasive resolution adopted by the Geneva World Economic Conference of 1927, and with the assistance of the study made of the problem and the draft prepared by the Economic Committee of the League of Nations, there was concluded on November 8, 1927, an international convention for the abolition of import and export prohibitions and restrictions. This agreement, although it was drawn in vague and ambiguous terms, and although it provided for many important exceptions and failed altogether to provide against indirect export controls through the use of export taxes, was nevertheless an important forward step. Some of the countries, however, made ratification by themselves conditional upon ratification by other specified countries, and the refusal of some of these countries, and especially Poland, to ratify within the specified time limit, has resulted in the failure of the convention to become operative.

Conferences held in 1928, also under League of Nations auspices, dealing with a special phase of the problem, namely, European export prohibitions and restrictions on hides and bones, had a more successful outcome. On September 11, 1929, seventeen European States signed the two conventions providing for the suppression of export duties and prohibitions on hides and bones, respectively, and also a special protocol stipulating that import duties on bones should not exceed stated maximum rates, and on October 1, 1929, these conventions became effective as between the signatory countries.

There have been several instances of suppression or prohibition of export restrictions being brought about by bilateral agreement between producing and consuming countries. In 1838 Sicily established a monopoly of sulphur, which promptly made a sharp increase in its price. The British Government protested, and after a sharp controversy of some duration, Sicily, in 1845, signed a treaty with Great Britain providing for the abolition of the sulphur monopoly in return for the surrender by Great Britain of her right under an earlier treaty to a reduction of 10 per cent in the Sicilian duties on her products. In the commercial treaties of 1911 and 1926 between Germany and Sweden, the latter country pledged herself not to prohibit the export of iron-ore to Germany. It was a characteristic of these treaties that they provided for a mutual exchange of considerations. Such was also the case in the hides and bones conventions of 1929, for the countries restricting the export of these commodities were also importers thereof and could accept the abolition of the export restrictions of other countries as adequate compensation for the suppression of their own restrictions. It is suggested that the lesson to be drawn from the successful conclusion of these treaties and conventions, as compared to the failure of the general convention of 1927, is that progress in securing the removal of export restrictions can be made only if, in return for their abolition, compensation of some sort is given to the countries which practice them. This can probably best be done through a series of bilateral treaties in which tariff or other concessions are the compensation for the removal of export restrictions. If the suppression of such restrictions on a large scale through a multinational agreement is to be obtained, it will probably prove necessary to make export restrictions only one of the matters dealt with in the general agreement, so that the countries desiring the removal of such restrictions may be able to offer, as inducement for their removal, reciprocal concessions of some other kind.

II

TARIFFS

By ANDRÉ SIEGFRIED

THE establishment of custom duties is the direct result of the autonomous conception formed by a country of its economic individuality. If the various states were to accept fully and without reserve a complete international division of industry, each one specialising in that which it can best produce or manufacture, there would be no need for customs. But all, or nearly all, the nations aim at the realisation of a certain economic independence; they delude themselves with the idea that they could live alone. Even though they know, fundamentally, the folly of such a programme, some sort of instinct drives them to follow it. Thus the political factor intervenes in tariff questions, side by side with strictly commercial interests; and thus arises the temptation to employ force—in other words, an eventual danger of war.

In the present state of international relations, it is difficult to deny to any country the right either to dispose of its products as it will, or to regulate its own markets. For these are among the most incontestable forms of national individuality and sovereignty. Until our conception of

sovereignty has been radically modified, none can
seriously take exception to the procedure with
regard to tariffs which is current, and almost
universal. The heated debates which have taken
place at Geneva, both over the international distribution of raw materials a dozen years ago, and
more recently over the tariff truce, prove without question that this aspect of individual sovereignty is one of those to which all States, both
great and small, cling most firmly.

The result is that we are always in a difficult
position when protesting against the tariffs of
others. We complain of the excessive duties imposed on our exports, yet ever tacitly admit that
a customs barrier is after all lawful. The tariff
cordon seems to be as natural as the police or
sanitary cordon; it is the logical, and therefore
the normal, consequence of the very existence of
States.

The indignation caused by protective duties
remains, as a rule, in the domain of economics;
it encroaches but rarely on the moral or political
domains, which is an undeniable mercy. "Tariff
wars", in fact, are not wars; they are fought with
duties, not with guns, for the most part.

The orthodox Free Trade school was, it is true,
more pessimistic, seeing in the Protectionist policy
an eventual, but direct, cause of war. It believed
that in breaking down tariff barriers we should
lay a solid foundation for the reign of peace.
Cobden and his disciples indeed looked upon
protective tariffs as something not only bad,
but wrong, and thought that humanity would be
morally uplifted by the complete abolition of all
economic barriers between nations.

This view, though now largely abandoned, still permeates the atmosphere, and has influenced our political outlook more than is realised. There are, indeed, many shame-faced Protectionists. Certain tariffs, for instance, are ostensibly labelled "fiscal"—that is to say, designed only to bring in funds to the Treasury—whereas they are really cleverly organised to defend national production against foreign competition. It is the same with the restrictions termed "sanitary", whose real object is quite other than sanitary, and which deceive no one. Transposing the remark of the moralist, we may say that such economic hypocrisy is nothing other than homage paid by Protectionist vice to Free Trade virtue. But the homage remains purely verbal.

It follows, naturally, that if economic interests were not able to rely upon the political support of the State, many sources of war would vanish. But unfortunately the trend of the twentieth century is not in this direction. Indeed, it must be admitted that this kind of Protectionist shame-facedness of which we have just spoken tends to become more rare, and looking back to the liberal tendencies of the nineteenth century, we find, from the economic point of view, a certain recoil of the international idea.

From these observations, it is perhaps possible to draw some practical lessons. Without doubt there will always be opposing interests in the world, but they will be less likely to give rise to war if we try to regulate them quite simply from the angle of, and according to the methods of, self-interest. The very fact of considering strictly economic rivalries in a strictly economic sense is

undoubtedly a guarantee against political complications. From this point of view, the international entanglement of private interests that
characterises our era is assuredly a factor for
peace. It is only when political or national passions are involved that the possibility of war
really arises.

Here we touch upon one of the most dangerous
causes of war—one which depends less upon the
opposition of interests than upon what may be
called the emotional conception of such interests
held by the Government or by public opinion.
Conflict at arms arises not so much from the dispute itself as from the passions that are enkindled
around it. It may be that in some cases Governments deliberately deceive the public in their
desire to provoke a conflict for other unadmitted
reasons. But it may also be that Governments are
themselves mistaken, and, self-hypnotised, adopt
extreme measures through a kind of auto-sugges-
tion of danger. In such a case the true cause of an
appeal to arms is chiefly psychological. We may
find an economic germ, but it can only develop
in virulent fashion in a political atmosphere. This
distinction is essential, because it enables us to
distinguish certain cases in which war might perhaps have been avoided, just as a legal process
can be avoided, through interest.

Since all States mutually recognise the right
to exist, and even the right to maintain existence
by those methods found to be most suitable, it
follows that a Protectionist policy cannot in itself
be considered liable to provoke war. To give
sufficient provocation the tariffs adopted would
have to be not only excessive—which does not

signify anything very definite—but also aggressive, and even aggressive towards some particular
country. Discrimination, in so far as it is not a
response, constitutes therefore the most harmful,
and eventually the most dangerous, element.

Now, to go further into details, let us consider,
from the point of view we are adopting, duties
on exports and duties on imports.

The free distribution of a country's natural
wealth entails the right to regulate exports—the
right to tax, to limit, or even to forbid the export
of such and such a product. If there is, however,
a monopoly of the producing country, and if there
exists also a principal buyer who cannot do without the product in question, we cannot deny that
the prohibition or even the limitation of export
might easily appear aggressive. And the injured
buyer might easily become subject to the impression of being hardly used and imposed upon.

Who can fail to recognise the gravity of such
a situation? Will not the purchasing State, if
powerful, be tempted to assure itself of the certain, durable, and even permanent distribution
of the product it fears to be deprived of? If it is
opposed by an export tax, a limitation, or worse
still an embargo, will it not intervene, by force
if necessary, in order to mitigate the severity of
the measures that injure it? Between the smallest
and most inoffensive export tax, and the total
prohibition of export, the whole scale of tariff
measures is conceivable; but also the whole scale
of methods of resistance, from the most courteous
protest to actual war. It might even be that the
purchasing State would be tempted to seize the
territory of the producing State, or—which comes

almost to the same thing—to establish a protectorate over it. In reality the whole question
would be one of rivalry for the control of raw
materials.

Where does right lie? It is very hard to say.
Given the accepted idea of independence, the
State which desires to retain the whole of the
raw materials that it produces is within its rights.
The younger countries, more and more, prefer to
export manufactured goods, and if it is a question of products that can be obtained elsewhere,
no serious political complications are to be feared.
But if it is a question of raw materials which
constitute a sort of monopoly, as, for example,
mineral wealth, it is obvious that the powerful
importing State is not likely to submit. Reason,
therefore, if not virtue, would counsel the less
powerful not to insist too much.

We may predict here the eventual and desirable formation of a code of economic international
good manners, which we may hope to see accepted by the strong as well as by the weak. We
must avoid confusing them with actual morals,
for they are, after all, conditioned by a wise
estimation of the forces to which they must submit, but there is nothing to prevent such true
begetters of peace from being recognised, codified,
and even guaranteed by an international consensus. The fine technical work that has been
started, in this respect, by the League of Nations
certainly moves in that direction.

Similar considerations suggest themselves with
regard to export rights or prohibitions, for the
problem is much the same. It is when they take
the form of obstacles to free importation that

tariffs generally arouse, in the Press or in public
feeling, the most bitter protests. Import duties
are, however, only indirectly aggressive, as a rule,
for the injured seller who complains of them can
always be advised to go and sell elsewhere. It
would be difficult for him to declare that he could
find no other market to replace the one lost to
him. Export may indeed be a vital necessity for
certain countries, but it is a world-wide necessity;
the right to export a specified product only to a
specified market can scarcely be claimed. For the
dispute to become embittered to the point of war,
it would be necessary, as indicated above, for the
closing of a particular market to affect directly
the essential interests of a particular country; it
would be necessary, in a word, for the repercussion
of the duty or the prohibition to be, not general,
but concentrated upon one special victim, thereby
comprising those elements of provocation and
discrimination upon the danger of which we have
already remarked. Between two countries of
equal strength, the result, at the most, would be
a tariff war—that is to say, peace would not be
threatened. But a powerful State opposed to a
weak one might be tempted to impose by force
the sales that the latter desired to prevent. The
history of colonisation furnishes more than one
example of such a conflict.

Nevertheless, the quarrel more often than not
takes the form of a business discussion. There
may be bitterness and even violence in the exchange of arguments, but usually the involving
of national honour, with the dangerous passions
that it unchains, is avoided; especially when the
tariff conflict is waged between countries of a

P

like state of civilisation—that is to say, when it is concerned solely with commercial interests. The contingency is more serious if, behind the exchange of merchandise which it is sought to regulate, two different civilisations, two different levels of life, affront and oppose one another. When American "machinery" is in conflict with European "quality", when Western industrialism, with its high standard of living, opposes the Asiatic proletariat, let us not be deceived into thinking that there is nothing more at stake than a simple question of tariffs. It is two different conceptions of life that oppose one another, and through this door there is a risk that political pressure may be brought into play.

Perhaps there is here no direct cause of war, but nevertheless the moral isolation invariably produced by widely differing social and economic standards is one of those unhealthy factors that tend to make more difficult the international co-operation necessary for peace.

We see that, in our present phase of human evolution, nations behave like biological organisms—that is, they are subject to the necessity of defending their existence. We cannot reasonably expect them to allow themselves to be guided exclusively by considerations of a moral order. The need for expansion—which we term Imperialism when it applies to others—is often merely the reaction of a being which seeks to preserve its own existence, and it is precisely when a country considers, rightly or wrongly, that its very existence is at stake, that the danger of war creeps in, and asserts itself, sometimes to the point of becoming irresistible. The country is very often wrong in its fears, and in such cases war should be avoidable—as it would be in many cases if we could eliminate the passionate affirmation of national individuality, and keep to a simple discussion of interests. For discussions of interests, in themselves, are in the end less dangerous than political discussions. Consequently, we ought, in the interests of peace, to treat business questions by business methods, and in limiting tariff controversies to their own territory we shall find the most effective means of preserving them from a bellicose atmosphere.

III

MIGRATION

By Moritz Bonn

I

In the early part of the nineteenth century, when modern business men began to enter into politics, the old-fashioned connection between war and wealth came to an end. For a long time the acquisition of wealth in its different forms had been one of the main objects of war, whilst its possession in the shape of land, treasure, and men, furnished the means to carry it on. The old connection between love and war, expressed in Greek folklore by the union of Mars and Venus, had long ago given way to a more recent connection between trade and war, between Mars and Mercury.

The advent of the Manchester School put an end to this conception. They advocated international relations unhampered by Government control, by doing business in such a way as to benefit both parties concerned. War to them was due to the greed of the feudal classes accustomed to get rich by spoiling weaker people, and to the duplicity of mean Governments, controlled by them. Protectionist tariffs and colonial expansion

were the last remnants of these dangerous
policies. Free Trade would do away with them by
bringing goodwill and peace to the nations of
the world; if they but followed modern conceptions of business war would practically be
abolished.

Very nearly a century has gone since the
modern business man discovered his call as
missionary of peace. Wars have been frequent
during this period; they certainly have not been
engineered by business men, as were some wars
in the eighteenth century; but, on the other hand,
they have not been prevented by pressure of
economic interests. Was this merely due to the
fact that few countries were ruled by business
men and none of them ruled by them exclusively?
Or was it because Free Trade had not been
adopted all over the world? Or was there perhaps
a weightier reason, namely—that nations are not
influenced exclusively by economic reasoning,
but swayed by nationalistic passions?

Whatever the explanation may be, it must
be openly acknowledged that neither economic
facts nor economic policies dealing with them
are always on the side of peace. For the mere
existence of private individuals, inoffensive,
well-meaning men, who mind their own business
and do not interfere in the nation's and the
world's affairs beyond addressing a Rotary Club
or a convention of their fellow-tradesmen, may
produce friction and international jealousy which
may end in war.

For there is one very important economic fact
which has been disturbing the equilibrium of
international relations for ever so long a time:

The economic resources of this world are not equally distributed amongst the different nations. The States composing the world, are divided in "Haves" and "Have-Nots". The Haves are often not as rich as the Have-Nots imagine them to be, and the Have-Nots are frequently not as poor as they pretend to be. But there is very considerable inequality, and the fear of discrimination arising from it is a grave menace to peace.[1]

II

An easy method to bring about a better relation between nationalities and opportunities might be found in a better distribution of population by means of migration.

Since religious persecution aiming at expulsion has practically come to an end, the migration movements, which have taken place on an enormous scale, originated mainly in an unequal distribution of natural wealth.[2] Countries with a

[1] Though density of population gives but a loose expression of the relation of natural resources of various countries to population, the differences are so great as to produce a very clear picture of the essentials of the problem.

Density of population per square mile:

Belgium . .	669	Union of South Africa	15·2
Great Britain .	480	Argentine . .	8·98
Germany .	347	Canada . . .	2·55
Indian Empire	177	Australia. . .	2·12
U.S.A. . .	40		

(From H. L. Wilkinson, *The World's Population Problems and a White Australia*, p. 8.)

[2] Political expulsion has, however, not ceased altogether. Millions of Russians have been driven from their country by the fear of Bolshevism. The treaties of Peace made the expulsion of German-born citizens in the annexed provinces of Poland compulsory, whenever they wished to maintain their German citizenship.

poor and dense population have always tried to
find room for the surplus by claiming a share in
the great undeveloped natural resources of the
world. This has been done in various ways. It
made primitive races search for better lands for
hunting, pasturing or farming, a search which was
the main cause of the incessant movements which
brought and bring them into conflict with other
tribes bent on the same purposes. The growth
of agriculture and stabilised settlements did not
put an end to these fluctuations. There are
always landless men—in a feudal age younger
sons unable to get an estate in their own countries, or small farmers or labourers who cannot
find land at home. The desire for land, or rather
for the space to live in, is one of the most potent
causes of friction and war through all the ages.
It has been the main motive spring for the
scramble for colonial annexations until the end
of the nineteenth century, when colonisation
practically came to a standstill. Scarcely any
vacant areas are left, and there is no no-
man's land which would-be emigrants could
conquer.

The rise of modern industry has merely shifted
the pressure. It has caused that phenomenal
growth of population which is the most characteristic feature of the nineteenth century. Land,
it is true, is no longer man's only source of wealth,
but industrial employment in old overpopulated
countries yields but low wages, thus making the
working class eager to emigrate to countries where
there are rich opportunities. The huge migration
movement of the nineteenth century was not so
much directed to newly acquired colonies, as to

the closer settlement of former dependencies, like
the United States or South America, or existing
dominions. From 1820 to 1927 the United States
alone received 37 million immigrants. In the early
years of the new century before the war the North
American continent swallowed up annually nearly
$1\frac{1}{2}$ million people. The hordes which moved across
the Atlantic in each year—the backward flow of
migrants from the United States or from the
Argentine was very considerable—were probably
far more numerous than the sum total of all tribes
roaming across Europe in the age which we call the
great migration of people ("Völkerwanderung").

III

This inflow of people constitutes a rather
clumsy and costly process of readjusting the distribution of the natural resources of the world
amongst the different nations of the earth. It
could not be completely successful. For the early
comers, under a system of private ownership of
land, naturally occupied the vantage points and
developed into a kind of economic aristocracy
whose growing wealth was dependent, however,
on the arrival of new immigrants. They were willing to pay these later immigrants much higher
wages than they had been receiving at home, but
they nevertheless did not admit them to a complete equality of income. Only in a few countries
like the United States, Canada, and in a different
way Australia and New Zealand, a land system
on a democratic basis was at last evolved, in such
a way as to make it fairly easy for the penniless
immigrant to become by and by a shareholder—

though in most cases a small shareholder—in the
natural wealth of these new countries.

As long as these resources seemed inexhaust-
ible, old settlers and later immigrants were always
willing to admit a new layer of more backward
immigrants, taking very little regard to racial
animosities and supposed racial inferiorities. For
after the first success was achieved or seemed
achievable, each stratum of immigrants was willing to rely for its further rise on the employment
of another wave of cheap immigrant labour. Only
after the country seemed fairly filled up, or after
a labouring class had been formed which insisted
on a settled standard of life, restriction of immigration set in. It really meant that the immigrant country was set on monopolising its
natural resources in the interest of its own settled
inhabitants. Under these circumstances, the right
to admission or non-admission of immigrants
which any sovereign State and any self-governing
colony may be inclined to exercise in the rather
narrowly conceived interest of their own people
is bound to become a source of friction which
may even lead to war.

IV

It is not merely the question of letting them in
or of keeping them out which may lead to trouble,
as was the case between the United States and
Japan after the Japanese "exclusion clause" of
the immigration restrictions Act of 1924. There
is besides the question of divided allegiance of
the immigrant between the country of his origin
and the country of his domicile. Whenever immigrants started from a country with a fairly

high civilisation to a country whose social, political, and economic conditions were very different or were even considered inferior to those of their home country, they did not assimilate to the populations of those new countries, provided they could settle down *en masse*. This had been the case of the German colonies settled in Russia in the eighteenth century. Where, on the other hand, the civilisation of the immigrant country is superior or considered superior to that of the emigrant country, where immigrants are admitted to full equal civil and political rights, complete assimilation seems possible in a rather short time; such was the case in the United States as long as the theory of the melting-pot prevailed. Complete assimilation to such a degree, however, that all memories, recollections and sympathies with the old country disappear is very rare indeed. And whenever there is a conflict between the two countries, the problem of double allegiance is bound to arise, as it did in the United States when the question of the hyphenated Americans cropped up. The fear of such dangers affects immigration policy considerably.

The Transvaal in Ohm Krueger's days was quite willing to admit Englishmen, but it was not willing to let them have votes, knowing their loyalty to the old country and fearing they might ultimately outvote the Boers. And the attitude of the Fascist Government which is trying to keep the Italian immigrants in France members of the Fascist State, has frequently strained Franco-Italian relations.

Social units, moreover, are not bound together merely by economic ties. Political, cultural, and

social values count for a lot. It is rather risky to
admit masses of political illiterates into a country
accustomed to self-government. If the immigrants
are admitted to political participation they are
expected to exercise an influence for which they
are not properly trained, a failure which may
greatly affect the future of the commonwealth if
they are numerous enough to decide issues. If they
are kept outside the political sphere and merely
admitted to civil, not to political rights, the nature
of the commonwealth is completely changed from
a democracy to an aristocratic ascendency based
on racial factors. The history of some of the
British colonies, like Jamaica, proves this clearly
enough. The slave trade and the influx of free
coloured people has so completely changed the
nature of society that the old forms of self-
government had to be restricted. Complete self-
government under an equal franchise of white
and coloured people would have meant the final
subjection of a small white minority to a coloured
majority.

Nor can the existence of widely different standards of comfort be neglected from an economic
point of view. The influx of an alien labouring
class with a low standard of living will in the
long run bring about low wages in all branches
of trade which it is fit to exercise. It will ultimately lower the standards of the superior race,
or drive it into some sort of non-economic defence. Its members will concentrate on skilled
trades and professions, to which artificially high
standards of payments will be attached. They
will maintain themselves within these sheltered
occupations not merely by their assumed superior

racial efficiency, but by legal or quasi-legal exclusions of their inferior racial competitors. The development of the labour problem in South Africa bears witness to the gravity of these problems.

V

Emigrant countries have often claimed that immigrant Governments are committing a serious wrong by creating a national monopoly for the benefit of their own people. Wherever the opportunities thus reserved exclusively remain undeveloped for want of a quickly increasing population, their owners are reproached with selfishness. As these vast areas are supposed to be held in trust for mankind in general, their masters are failing it by not developing them themselves, and by not letting in other people who would be willing to do so.

It can be argued, of course, that such a policy of retarding a country's natural development by preventing immigration may be short-sighted; it may lead indirectly to very unpleasant consequences, such as accelerating superfluous competitive industrialisation of densely populated countries which must give work to their people at any price. But as long as economic altruism is not the settled policy of emigrating countries, they can scarcely press for its adoption by immigrating countries.

Moreover, the most obvious obstacles to a fairly equal distribution of population all over the world must be sought less in the nationalistic attitudes of different Governments than in the existence of varied races and nationalities

who follow widely diverse ways of living and have
greatly divergent views of life. Essential differences in cultural standards, in religious outlook,
in political training, and in economic efficiency
cannot be done away with by being ignored or
by being called prejudices.

Mankind, no doubt, it can be said, learns very
quickly. It is fairly easy to raise to higher levels
a comparatively small number of people who may
be called backward (from various points of view)
when compared to the people who admit them
to their country. This can only be done by mix-
ing them completely with their hosts and teachers.
Such mixture and the results of it are mainly a
question of proportion. A handful of foreigners,
whatever their standards may be, can easily be
assimilated by any race, provided both parties
are willing to do so. The physical and psychological consequences of such a mixture will be
negligible when a mere handful of individuals is
being amalgamated. The problem becomes very
different when it is a question of big numbers.
A huge mass of alien immigrants cannot be assimilated completely in a short time by any
population without leaving its marks on the
future type, whether for good or for evil. Such a
process of assimilation must always take a very
long time, even if both component elements are
willing to undergo it.

VI

I am not at all sure whether the peace of the
world would be better served if immigrant countries widely opened their gates to admit the
flood from all corners of the world which people

want to leave in the hope of bettering themselves. The result might not only be overcrowding in relation to the available natural resources
of the new countries but a kind of torpor in the
old countries. What is worse, the truth of the
well-known proverb "Familiarity breeds contempt" might be proved anew. The place of a
more or less academic antagonism which may
exist between two countries on account of
Government restrictions of immigration might
be taken by actual race riots between different
population groups who meet in the struggle for
life's opportunities and do not like or understand
each other.

As long as the Negro population of the United
States was mainly restricted to the South, the
North proclaimed its belief in complete equality.
The few members of the race who strayed across
the border-line were fairly well received, if full
regard is taken of the difference in their social
standards and their existing status. Since Negro
quarters have arisen in the great cities of the
North, racial fights, with all the brutality un-
avoidable from them, have often taken place, even
during the period of prosperity when the Negro
has not ousted the white man. Where legal dis-
qualifications are considered unfair, economic
competition may be added to racial animosities,
and cohabitation of different races may be anything but desirable. We must not forget that
many modern wars have been the outcome of
nationalism. This nationalism was due in most
cases to the compulsory cohabitation of various
races. Racial conflicts have occasionally been
settled by federated constitutions and large

measures of autonomy. But in other cases the problem has merely been changed, not solved: masters have been made serfs, when serfs have become masters. Most of these problems originated in some form or other of migration; it might have been better for both sides, if these migrations had not taken place.

It may be all very well to let immigration come in freely as long as there is a chance for every newcomer. But when things are getting settled and when opportunities are getting scarce, restriction of immigration and control at the frontiers may in the long run better serve the cause of peace than an inefficiently supervised rush for new lands.

When restrictions are conceived in a spirit of international fairness, when they are not couched in the language of national arrogance, by which a race fearful of maintaining its position is trying to exclude its ablest competitors by branding them morally as inferiors, misunderstandings can be avoided. Friction is due far more to methods of unfair arrogance and to indecent application of what might be decent laws than to the mere economic fact of control. The immigration restrictions by which the different self-governing members of the British Empire protect themselves against unrestricted immigration from the mother country have not endangered the framework of the British Empire. This shows plainly enough that economic caution need not produce political friction. Manners, after all, count for something in the economic world as well as measures.

Whatever is done in this way and by whichever

method it may be done, the fact remains that economic inequality existing between the various countries of the world can scarcely be abolished by mass migration. Something, no doubt, will be achieved by the variations in the rate of increase of the population in the various countries. But the natural increases of thinly settled countries like the United States or Australia are fairly low, and the rates of the thickly settled countries like England or Germany have only lately fallen below them. It would take a very long time before even the roughest equalisation of inequality of resources could be brought about in this way. So the danger due to inequality of natural resources is bound to remain if it cannot be mitigated by economic policy, by lowering trade barriers, and by enabling the more densely populated countries to participate in the world's wealth by participation in international exchange.

IV

ECONOMIC OCCASIONS OF CONFLICT
IN THE FAR EAST

By W. J. HINTON

(1) *Eastern Siberia, Mongolia, Manchuria*

Here is a region of competitive Russian, Chinese, and Japanese penetration and immigration. The final composition of the racial map is uncertain, especially in Outer Mongolia, but it seems certain that the Chinese strain will predominate in Inner Mongolia and Manchuria. This is bound to make the present Japanese political ascendancy in those regions more difficult to maintain. Japan has thus a problem of withdrawal to face some time in the future, and this is likely to lead to conflict.[1]

[1] The above words were written before the outbreak of the armed conflict in Manchuria and Shanghai, but they may stand. Essentially Japan's problem in China is one of withdrawal, as Britain's was in Egypt and is now in India. But withdrawal is difficult.

Russia took, by settlement and diplomatic chicanery, some 350,000 square miles of what was once Manchuria: but this was in 1860, and to-day nobody considers Amuria and the Maritime province as anything but integral parts of the Russian lands. Japan did not demand the actual cession of almost empty lands in Manchuria, to which she had as much, or as little, right as Russia to Amuria. But she did secure a position of temporary

The situation in Eastern Siberia is not yet
developed, but in Outer Mongolia the U.S.S.R.
has secured control. If the Chinese immigrate
thither in large numbers they will create a political problem—but the U.S.S.R. by its policy of
local cultural nationalisms may be able to find a
place in its system which will satisfy the Mongols
and immigrant Chinese. Also, it is not likely to
suffer the immigration to proceed to such a point
as to cause trouble.

In this same region the Japanese and Russians
dispute from time to time about the Okhotsk
fisheries and the Sakhalien oil-fields. Access to
both of these is very important for Japan. As she
has to rely more and more upon her fisheries to
feed her increasing population, she would probably go to great lengths for the former of these
two rights. These are actual issues of the moment,
but a peaceable settlement has been reached for
the present. When Eastern Siberia fills up and
industrialises, the questions will arise again.

control by her acquisition of the South Manchurian Railway
from Russia.
    Since then she has halted between two opinions. In 1915 she
took the high hand, and advanced on the road to making Manchuria a protectorate on the model of the French and British
protectorates in the Indies. In 1921–22 the opposite party was
in the ascendant, and in their Washington policy attempted to
undo the harm of the Twenty-one Demands. But the Chinese
were not satisfied, and, with the development of non-co-opera-
tion and boycott, as well as the mere disorder of bad and corrupt
government, the friendly gesture has failed. Japan is now upon
the other tack, and in spite of European and American opposition, has established a virtual protectorate in Manchuria. But
even if she reduces Manchuria and Mongolia to order for a
generation, she will be confronted again and again with opposition of the kind which Britain, for all her experience, meets in
India. Thus, sooner or later, the withdrawal must come. The
alternative would seem to be to conquer and hold down all
China, a task which is probably impossible even if she were
left alone by the world to do it. (Feby. 1932.)

(2) *The Japanese Archipelago*

The land available for food cultivation being very limited, and emigration being no sufficient remedy, as well as distasteful to the Japanese, there is a dilemma: either artificial restriction of population or further industrialisation. The latter is at present the only feasible course in practice. It involves access to raw material markets in the mainland, both in Manchuria and in the Yangtze, and in India and the East Indies. It also involves access to markets for raw silk in the U.S.A. and textiles and hardware throughout the East and Africa, but especially in China and India. In both India and China economic nationalism is growing, and the types of goods now manufactured by the Japanese will be the first excluded by protective measures, as they can be made, and not always less efficiently, in those two countries. Thus Japan will find herself in a position similar to that of Great Britain, obliged to rely upon the export of services and high grade goods and other methods of avoiding tariff barriers, or to control markets such as Manchuria by political force. It is doubtful whether the political ideals and tendencies of this century are favourable to States of the type of Britain and Japan, Belgium and Holland, dependent upon world trade and international intercourse. If the course of evolution is towards the State of sub-continental size, Japan will have to throw in her lot with one of the mainland States. She may thus be obliged to force herself upon China. If her position became bad enough to lead to revolution, which is not quite impossible, then she might join the Russian system. In the absence of a complete, and most unlikely, change of policy in the matter of international trade by most nations on the Pacific, this is a real, though distant, possibility.

(3) *China*

The central region of the coast of the Far East, China, is constantly the theatre of wars. It is a mistake to regard these as mere civil tumults or armed general elections. They grow more costly in lives as time goes on. Moreover, there is a large territory in which Communist armies are operating. The situation may be compared to that of Germany during the Thirty Years' War. The economic occasions of these conflicts is the opportunity of enrichment presented by military occupation of towns and territories, and their exploitation by taxation, or, as an alternative, looting. The absence of alternative forms of exploitation and occupation for the organisers and soldiers is due to the backwardness of Chinese capitalism. This, again, is now due less to mental conservatism than to the lack of security for life and property—thus completing the vicious circle. The partial development of a capitalist economy under the political protection of the foreigners led to an increase in the wealth of the larger cities. It is not certain how far the parasitic activities of the soldiers have destroyed this wealth, but it is clear that the disorganisation of the country increases the risk of economic catastrophe as a result of famines caused by flood or drought. The peasantry are rather worse off than they were under the Empire, and there is

an increasing probability of a Jacquerie or a
Communist civil war. The prime causes are, as
always, ethical, not economic. A well governed
China could support double its present population on its present territory at the present low
standard. It is congested rather than generally
overpopulated.

(4) *The East Indian States of the south*

In the East Indian States of the south the most
probable causes of conflict are connected with the
revolt of native mixed populations against the
tutelage of the white imperialist powers, and are
therefore not mainly economic. The Philippino
revolt against Spain and the subsequent revolt
against American rule, breaking down into pro-
longed political agitation, is the best known example. There are less marked movements in the
Netherlands East Indies, and much feebler movements in French Indo-China and British Malaya.
In Burma, which belongs to this region, the revolt is much stronger, but is partly economic in
character. Some racial feeling is introduced in
Burma and Siam by dislike of the immigrant
Indians, as well as Chinese.

In these movements there are economic elements. The Chinese as middlemen sometimes
exploit the natives very severely. Yet in British
Malaya and in Java the Malays have, on the
whole, been tolerant of the influx of the Chinese.
In British Malaya there are signs of strong feeling
among the Chinese settlers for their Chinese home-
land, but it would require very little to make
them enthusiastic citizens of a Malayan Dominion.
Their mentality is very similar to that of the

European immigrant into America who entered
the country poor and has "made good". Antagonism to the Chinese is largely due to economic
causes. They become a kind of middleman caste
between the brown native and the white mer-
chant, banker, or ruler. This leads to jealousy on
the part of the brown native. Then they become
larger capitalists, and jealousy appears among
the white ruling class. Educated members of the
local races are apt to regard the beneficial economic development of these regions (by large
capital investments leading to large exports of
plantation products) as exploitation of the
brown man by the white, which indeed it may
become.

The rise of nationalism in these regions
must lead to. conflicts similar in character to,
though less acute than that now occurring in
India. As in other regions of predominantly agricultural character, the recurrent sudden falls in
the value of their main productions, both absolutely and relatively to the manufactured goods
they consume, intensifies the strain of all the
above antagonisms.

In general, there is nothing in the basic economic conditions which would make war, or even
serious conflict, *inevitable* in any of these areas,
if men were rational. As they are not, their illusions as to their national economic advantages
will doubtless lead to the same conflicts as
economic nationalism and imperialism have led
to elsewhere. These conflicts will be embittered
by class and race hostilities, which are being
deliberately exacerbated by those interested in
revolution on the Russian model. Obviously the

only hope is in movements which strengthen both goodwill and understanding, and of these the former is perhaps the more essential, as it makes the latter possible. In this task the religious leaders may do much to help.

INDEX

THE END